An Uncommon Friendship

A memoir of mental illness, love, and friendship

Monique Colver

with

Stewart Young

COLVER PRESS

Cover design by Susan Veach

Cover photo by Jodi Tripp

ISBN: **0615638473**
ISBN-13: **978-0615638478**

DEDICATION

This book is dedicated to those who live with mental illness, wherever you are, and those who love them.

You are not alone.

Contents

ACKNOWLEDGMENTS

None of this would have been possible without the love and support of the following family and friends. My husband, Andrew Colver, who understood how important it was for both of us to take care of Stew. Stew Young, my co-author, who always encouraged me to get this done, even when he had more important things on his mind, like dying. Stew's parents, Roberta and Ken Young, who were always supportive and loving. My editor, Karen Adams, who looked at my hodgepodge of an original manuscript and didn't run screaming. Instead, she provided a framework for the material that did something I had trouble with: she made it make sense. Robin Rutherford and SarahAnne Hazlewood, my matrons of honor, who greatly helped my assimilation back into society. All my friends, including especially the members of my own personal Internet Ax Murderers Club. You have all been invaluable and a great source of joy. You know who you are.

This book includes essays and journal entries by both Monique and Stewart Young, and I have attempted to make it clear who is writing when. Any misstatements or confusion in that regard is solely my responsibility.

Monique Colver

INTRODUCTION

When we met, I was thirty-nine and he was twenty-six. I was married, and though I told people I was happily married, it was a bit of a lie. I wasn't unhappily married, but mostly alone married, resigned to a life of living alone with another person in the house. My husband of almost twenty years had stopped drinking, again, and when he wasn't drinking he spent hours brooding and smoking cigarettes, sitting alone in the garage or outside.

This was a big improvement from when we lived in the Midwest and he'd sit by the fireplace (because one can't sit outside in the winter) and build colossal sculptural beer-can masterpieces on the hearth. He'd blow his cigarette smoke towards the fireplace so he could say to me, "You can't possibly have a problem with my smoke because it's all going up the chimney," though his version wasn't as grammatically correct. But it wasn't. The room filled with smoke, my eyes watered, and he'd continue drinking until there was no option but for him to stumble off to bed, rank with the smell of sweat and beer and cigarettes.

Good times.

On Saturdays, in the Midwest, he'd take my car under the guise of getting it washed. He'd leave about lunch time and return shortly after two a.m., once all the bars were closed. Sometimes the car would be clean, sometimes not, but he'd always be tanked. Once or twice, when I responded badly to his drinking, he chased me and grabbed me by the throat, and he held me down, and it was at those times that I knew that I was stupid for hanging in there. But at some point all of it had ceased to matter to me, and I no longer expected him to be around when he said he would be. Lying was second nature to him.

And when we moved, yet again, back to California, he promised he'd stop drinking and he'd help around the house for a change, and even help with my writing business, but as usual he didn't mean any of it, and when we got to California he didn't help at all. In the winter, in the rain, he came home from work at the end of the day and plopped himself on the couch in front of the TV, and when I came home later, wet and tired from a long day temping in an office, he'd raise one arm half-heartedly from the couch — his special greeting for me — and when I asked if he wanted to give Rex, the diabetic dog, his insulin shot, he'd wave his arm again and say, quite nonchalantly, "No, you can do it," as if bestowing upon me a favor.

And so I would. I didn't mind giving Rex his shot, or feeding the dogs — Rex and the three girls, Allie, Jesse, and Tash — I loved them more than I loved my husband. In the Midwest, I often fantasized about leaving him, about putting the dogs in the truck one Saturday afternoon when he was out "washing my car" and driving all of us, four dogs and me, to someplace where we could start over and no one would find us, at least not anyone I knew, but I never knew where to go. I knew this was just a fantasy, the kind of thing one saw only in the movies, never in real life. And so I didn't go, but stayed.

After I'd fed the dogs and paid attention to them, I'd give him his dinner — he did not cook nor even pretend he could take care of himself — and then I'd take my dinner (probably something different than his, because I was so weary of the unvaried meat and potatoes diet he subsisted on) back to the bedroom where I could be alone because even when he was in the same room, I was still alone.

But I wished, sometimes, that he'd make an effort to act as if he cared.

When spring came he spent all his time outdoors, building a fence and brooding about the sadness of his life, but at least he wasn't always in front of the TV. When he was, I was back in the bedroom or in my office above the garage. I knew this was the way it would continue, though occasionally I'd say something like, "Someday I'll leave and find someone who appreciates me," but he'd only grunt, because he didn't believe it and he knew I didn't either. Who else would want me? No one, that's who. At least this way I had my dogs, and I had security, and if that wasn't enough, I still had my dogs. They are repeated because they were the one reason I'd stay, they meant more to me than leaving.

And that is exactly when I met Stewart Young, who was twenty-six, single and unattached, funny and smart, and my life would never be the same.

An Uncommon Friendship

CHAPTER 1

Blood slowly dripped down his arm, surprising us both. This is the moment that stays with me, that one morning in October of 2002, when I realized we were really in trouble. This was no minor depression that Stew could fight off, and though there would be far worse episodes, it was the sight of the blood that told me that our life had changed, and things were only going to get worse.

This is our beginning, the start of it all, the only point I know how to begin. It's not the conventional way to start a love story, I know. It's hard to start anywhere, in fact, because time and experience colored everything that came afterwards. And starting here, of course, prompts questions like, "Was he like that when you married him?"

People ask me that. I don't know why. It would be the ultimate in the "Can I change my man to make him the way I want him?" contest, for sure. When I met him he was funny and smart and motivated. He had a history of depression, but who doesn't? Yes, I'm quite aware there are a few people who don't, but that's more of the exception than the rule, at least in my experience. Perhaps I need to travel in new circles. But in my world — the people I grew up with, the friends I have — if you throw a rock in any direction you'll hit someone with depression or anxiety. Please don't take that literally. The last thing a depressive needs is someone throwing rocks at them.

But no, he was not like that when I met him. I'm not quite that anxious to prove myself by remaking a person, and I certainly wouldn't think it within my power. (I tried that with my first husband for twenty years and learned my lesson.) It became obvious early on that there were certain behaviors that were troubling, but they were merely idiosyncrasies then. He'd told me his stories, as we all tell each other our stories in the beginning. He'd had bouts of depression and anxiety, and when he'd lived alone in San Diego for a short time he'd had a very hard time with it, and had been brought home again, not finishing the education he'd been there for. No big deal, no one's perfect, and I have my own troubling behavior to deal with, so I don't point fingers at anyone. I'm a long-time depressive with occasional bouts of mania, and I consider it a matter of course. Simply, Stew made me laugh, something I was in desperate need of. Forget about stunning good looks and fat wallets — if you can make me laugh, I'm yours. I like nothing more than to be entertained, and a quick wit plus intelligence are sure winners. That, and I was so comfortable with Stew. We were best friends first, and there's no better foundation to start with.

I met him in February 1997, when I was pretty damn disgusted with my life but also determined to make some changes. My temp job had become overwhelmingly annoying. I'd taken it just so my husband and I could close on the house we'd bought, and it was tedious and there were lots of complaining customers. At the same time, I was ramping up my writing business, such as it was, which at the time consisted mostly of every-other-week columns in the Air Force Times. So one day I quit the temp job, just walked away from it as if I hadn't a care in the world. I'm often impetuous in my decisions.

My husband had little reaction to this news. By this time he had little reaction to anything that went on around him. I joined the Chamber of Commerce and after my first breakfast I knew I needed help with public speaking. Truthfully, I'd known it long before then. I've always been painfully shy. I don't like talking to groups of people at all. My discomfort is obvious, and at that first breakfast the guy next to me — an older man with a Howdy Doody face — told me I should go to Toastmasters, and that it would really help me.

It's all about selling out there in business, which is hard to do if one doesn't want to talk to anyone. Knowing that, I went to my first Toastmasters meeting early one morning determined to learn something useful. If you've never been to Toastmasters, I can tell you that generally people are friendly. There's a format to follow, and rules, and the Howdy Doody guy, whose name was Stu, introduced me to a few people. One of the people he introduced me to was Stew Young, who was on the schedule to speak.

Stew was a big guy, by which I mean: He was heavy. I hesitate to say fat because no one wants to be called fat. But he was big, with shoulder-length curly hair, and young. He had kind brown eyes, the right eyelid a bit droopy, and glasses. He was no one's idea of a knight in shining armor, which would have been a tight fit anyway, but I've never been big on looks. Looks don't tell me anything about a person, it's only what people came with when they started, it's not as if it tells me anything at all.

Stew's speech was about being prepared, or something like that, and he started off ponderously, telling us how important it is to be prepared, both mentally and physically. And then he started looking around, as if confused, and told us he had to go get something out of his truck, and he'd be right back. He started for the door with his shambling walk, and then started half-running, as if hoping we wouldn't notice his rushing. He came back in then, a sheaf of papers in his hand, and headed back to the lectern. By this time we were all laughing, not nervously in that way people do when they're not sure what to do, but uproariously, delightedly. He completed his speech as if not noticing how much fun we were having, and received a good bit of applause.

After the meeting Stu asked if I'd like to come have breakfast with him and Stew, and since I had nowhere else to be, I went. Most people had to go to work, but the three of us had no work. Stu and Stew were working on their own project, and I had nothing, just a fledgling writing business and an idea of what I wanted to do.

I found them great fun to talk to, especially Stew, as we talked excitedly about things like logos and business card formats. This may not seem interesting to most people, but I'm uncomfortable talking about myself, and I'm a weird that way, so it worked.

And by "worked" I mean that Stew was just so easy to talk to and so interested in who I was. He was easygoing and he made me laugh. My husband was not easy to talk to. We'd taken different paths, and while I'd finished college he'd studied drinking extensively. He often didn't get what I was talking about, and often wanted me to explain things to him. I don't remember what things, but I didn't care for the role of teacher. I found it exhausting.

Stew made me feel young again, and he helped me break out of my self-imposed prison. I was lonely in my marriage, and Stew was my friend from day one. I'd ask my husband to go places and do things with me, but his answer was always no. No, no, no. And so I turned to my new best friend.

I thought that's all it would be. For one thing, there was the thirteen-year age difference. And there was the marriage thing, which I was still taking seriously as a condition of being a grown-up. I came from a family of multiple marriages, of mixed and matched partners and children, and I thought that by sticking with my original plan I'd be doing something right. But we were living parallel lives, my husband and I, and though I did not realize it, I was ripe for a change. I was still thinking that it was the right thing to do, to stick in there, and act as if it all made sense somehow.

Then Stew and I met by chance and fell madly in like with each other.

We started spending more time together. He and Stu drafted me into their project, and so the three of us would meet often, but then Stu became irrelevant. And a bit annoying, being an annoying sort of person. Stew gave me hope that I could make my life better, and he believed in me like no one else ever had. That's rather important, isn't it? He thought I could do anything I wanted, and I couldn't resist.

We fell in love like giggling teenagers, snatching time here and there, and when I realized what had happened I had to tell my husband. I could not deceive him, it wasn't fair, and it was obvious something had to change.

He did not take it well. Why should he? It was an ugly end to a long union. For twenty years we'd stuck together, and though I'd become unhappy in my married aloneness and would often tell him that someday I'd find someone else, neither of us believed it. When I did find someone else, he still didn't believe it. It was one of the worst things I've ever had to do, and it was made worse when he wouldn't let me leave the house and took my phone away. He kept me there overnight, a prisoner, alternately angry and hurt, and he raped me because he was mad and I was still, according to him, his property. I felt so much guilt that I never named the incident until many years later, just locked it away as a bad memory. Still, I always deeply regretted the sadness I caused him. It was my fault. I shouldn't have done it like that. I should have left the marriage first, and then found someone else.

But I'd never thought it was possible. I never knew that I had options. I told everyone who asked that everything was fine, because what kind of person talks about the trouble in their marriage?

I was released the next morning, and I drove away with my computer and some clothing, my cell phone restored to me. I cried, sad that I'd hurt him and missing my dogs. A better person would have stuck it out, would not have strayed. I was selfish and I knew it. I had so much guilt that when it came time to divvy up the marital assets, I made no claim on his military retirement. When he wanted a lawyer to tell him what else he could get from me, the lawyer said, "Be very nice, because she's giving you a great gift." So he eased up a bit, fortunately, for he'd cut off all my funds when I left. He said I could have nothing, and I had to leave behind my dogs, but when he realized that meant he had to take care of the big ol' house and four dogs on his own, he relented. Well, what he actually did was call me and say that since obviously neither of us could take care of the dogs he was going to have them put to sleep. I threatened to rip his head off if he hurt one hair on any of my dogs. I myself couldn't have done that, of course, but Stew and his friends could. So he decided to move out of the house and leave it and the dogs to me. I later lost the house in foreclosure, but it was the dogs that mattered to me anyway.

Before this, I'd always judged people who cheated. "Why don't they just leave the marriage first?" I'd wonder. "It's not right," I'd say. I was deeply shocked to find I was capable of the very thing I'd condemned. So I had to change my opinion. I couldn't very well continue to condemn the same thing I was guilty of, could I? Things happen, despite our best intentions. I wish I'd had the courage to change my life before Stew came along, that I could have gone out on my own, but I didn't. Stew saved me long before I saved him.

I think that's how these things happen sometimes. We can't imagine other options, other choices, and then they pop up in front of us and we're so relieved that we just go ahead and take the fork in the road. (If there's a fork in the road, of course you're going to take one or the other. Or stand at the crossroads, dithering, and there's no future in that.)

So I looked for a job, and Stew's parents welcomed me into their home until I could get a place of my own. They welcomed me as if I were deserving of acceptance, and Stew and his family were so supportive of me that I immediately felt like I was part of the family.

I found a job, but instead of moving into an apartment I moved back into my house, and Stew moved in with me and the dogs. My soon-to-be ex had always left much of the home and dog maintenance to me, not wanting to deal with it, but I was more than happy to.

I worked on developing a friendly relationship with him, and occasionally, before he moved out, when I was staying with Stew's parents, he'd ask me to come over and make him something to eat. He was hopeless. The man would starve to death before he'd make the effort to learn how to cook.

Sometimes the husband would pick me up at work and take me to lunch. He was still angry, but I wanted a peaceful divorce. For one thing, it's cheaper. For another thing, why not? I didn't want anything from him. I only wanted us to go our separate ways. Sure, I could've used half his retirement, and I was "entitled" to it, but I didn't want it. What does entitlement have to do with anything anyway?

So the divorce proceeded and Stew and I and the dogs learned to live together, and we just kept having fun. I remember looking out our large windows that overlooked the valley while he held me, and life was just so good. We could do anything we wanted, and for the first time in many years — maybe in my entire life — I started to believe in myself, and in having choices.

Except for the money thing, of course. Stew had no income, and I had a job that wasn't exactly well-paying, and we had a huge house payment. But we were happy, and we knew things would get better.

Stew and I married shortly after my divorce was final. This was in northern California, but not the part of northern California with the temperate climate, nor the part of California with a healthy economy. Instead, the heat was oppressive and the economy depressing. Neither of us liked the heat much. I'd been reluctant to return to California at all, one reason being the heat, the other being my Samoyed dogs, who did not like the heat. But my ex had wanted to, and he had military orders sending him there because that's what he had asked for — he'd always thought the next move would be the one to make him happy, and it never was. He suffered greatly from the-grass-is-always-greener syndrome so I'd followed him for years, whether I liked it or not.

One hot summer day, several months after our wedding, while Stew and I were sitting at Der Wienerschnitzel (it had air conditioning, and we were in danger of expiring from the heat), one of us said, "Hey, why don't we just head north?" It seemed so logical. Business was going nowhere, we couldn't afford the overpriced house I'd been "awarded" in the divorce, and we were hot. Stew was a big guy, and he hated the heat. I got sick a lot, in the heat, and we were miserable. Cooling our monstrous-sized house with air conditioning was cost prohibitive too, especially since my accounting job wasn't bringing in nearly enough money. Stew had been unemployed when I met him, and he kept our writing business going while I went to my job every day. We were broke, and we were hot.

"Seattle," we said, "There's a place that's more to our liking!"

We knew no one in Seattle, but we saw no problem with that. As a former military wife I was used to moving to different places, and, in fact, often felt like I had to get going after a few years, more to keep getting a fresh start than anything else.

So in October of the year we married, we left northern California and headed farther north. We had no jobs, little money, and at the time we decided to move, we had four dogs to contend with. Between the time we decided to go and the time we left we lost three of the dogs, to age and heat and strokes and diabetes. They'd been my life, these dogs, and so we packed up the ashes of the three dogs, the one remaining dog, Jesse, and everything we could fit into a big rented truck, and we headed north.

Stew's best friend, Jake, and Stew's dad, Ken, made the trip up with us, to help us get set up on the other end. I drove alone in my car with Jesse, which meant I wasn't alone at all, and Ken drove the U-Haul while Stew and Jake drove Stew's truck. We arrived at the end of a long day the first of October, and I looked at the house we'd rented and felt as if it were wrong, the house. I felt uncomfortable in it, but it had a fenced back yard for the now-one dog, and we thought it would be okay. I chalked it up to the cheapness of the construction. I was used to well-made houses and this one was obviously built to be nothing more than a rental. I'm a snob, but I'm working on it.

I recommend this sort of upheaval for people who want a change, by the way. Take a risk, try something new, just get out there and go. I've been told this is foolhardy and dangerous, but we had a rented house to move into — we'd thought ahead that much — and what else did we need? I'd never had a problem getting a job, and this was prior to the Great Recession.

A day after moving in, I was driving Jake (who is legally blind so he doesn't drive), to see his mother, who lived nearby. Heading down the main street in Everett, we were struck by an underage unlicensed driver coming from a side street. This was clearly an omen of worse things to come, though I didn't see it. Brand new to town, and I have an accident? What sort of sign do I need? How much more obvious can you get? My back and neck were injured, just enough so I couldn't go to work immediately because of the pain. We sent Jake and Stew's dad home, and Jake was okay after a bit of physical therapy. So was I, eventually. Physically, at least.

Naturally life did not settle down easily after that. In California we'd had a writing business but our major clients had been left behind, so I took temp accounting assignments while figuring out what to do. So did Stew, who was good at temp jobs. Seattle was supposed to be a new start for us, the beginning of a grand adventure. We were optimistic, somewhat naively no doubt, but for twenty years I'd moved whenever my husband was transferred and the thought of starting over didn't scare me. We could both work, I'd always been able to get work, and we weren't afraid of the future.

Well, maybe just a bit. There's always a bit of fear with change, even if we expect the change to be good. It's still change. It's still a stressor, and it's still something to adapt to. Adapting requires a certain skill set: flexibility, optimism, a willingness to work hard at creating a different life. Stew had the optimism and he was willing to work hard, but he wasn't as flexible as I was with change.

And while I temped and eventually accepted a full-time job, Stew accepted a job which was successful only in increasing his stress. He worked on the floor of a large home electronics store, interacting with people and customers and meeting sales quotas and all kinds of things which are a pain in the butt. If you've ever worked retail, you know what I mean. The company promoted the sale of warranties, which, as we all know, are often worthless, but it's how they made their money. It's not the margin on the products that makes money; it's the warranties that bring in the dough.

That company, as far as I can tell, has gone out of business. "Yay!" to that, I say. I can't forgive them for causing Stew so much stress and for making such demands on him. It started his downward decline, I think. That, and being suddenly responsible, with a wife and a dog and all the trappings of adulthood. He'd felt bad in the big house in California, because he hadn't felt he'd earned any of it. Responsibility had never really been his thing, as I was to discover. He could fake it pretty well, but he really wasn't into it.

Stew was not aggressive, he was not a salesman, he was quiet and self-effacing, polite and honest. It wasn't a good fit, and he doesn't do well with pressure. I couldn't even tell you exactly what happened first. I'd come home to find he had, instead of going to work, gone to the ER for suicidal ideation (which means he'd been considering suicide as a viable option.) He'd try to take care of it himself so it wouldn't alarm me. He scheduled counseling, but it was faith-based and while Stew was very faith-based altogether, it didn't work for him. He started collecting the little ID bands that ERs strap on when one checks in. He was severely depressed. I attempted the normal wifely cheering up. I was not unfamiliar with the feeling that the pain would stop only if one could remove oneself from the world, which is a nice way to say I could understand, having dealt with it myself, the lure of suicide as being a good idea. Nothing overtly psychotic had come up yet — just pain and depression and anxiety — a natural byproduct for Stew, and he kept trying to be what he imagined as normal.

Then he quit that job. That helped, it relieved him of the stress, and he went back to temping. Things were looking up again.

He got another job, in an office. He started as a temp, and then temped elsewhere, and then when the office had an opening he was hired on permanently. It was all very normal and very social. He had a job that appealed to his analytical nature and he was well-liked. He had friends there, though he bemoaned the fact that he was surrounded by older women, for the most part. But he got along with them well. I was, after all, an older woman, and he got along with me just fine.

We moved from our house when a drain flooded the downstairs, which was our office space (for the fledgling and flailing writing business we insisted we had.) The landlord dragged his feet in getting it cleaned up and blamed our dog for the problem. The matter ended up in small claims court, and while I just wanted to move on and forget about it, Stew insisted we fight it, which added another layer of stress. He obsessed about it at great length. It was unhealthy, I could see that, but I couldn't stop it. We lost in court partly because, the judge said, "Californians come up here and think they can get away with anything." Stew was so angry. He couldn't let things go anymore. I worried about him. The court case had become such an obsession, and while I wanted to just drop it, he insisted we fight it. We had a new, better, place to live, and I just wanted to go forward. But he couldn't let go.

The ability to let go is, I think, a great indicator of good mental health. I'm no expert, but I've had poor mental health and I've had good mental health, and when I can let things go and move on I've been happier.

While he was working his way through his job and seeming to come out of his depression, I accepted a position with a company that didn't interest me, but it was a steady paycheck. (I walked out after a couple of years, a bold move when I needed the income, but I despised my manager more.) During the time I worked there I developed fibromyalgia, characterized by pain, exhaustion, and an inability to be as effective as I'd like at anything at all.

We stumbled through the next couple of years, attempting equilibrium, and things were good when his job, his real job, first started. He was happy, mostly, occasionally depressed, but okay. I left my job when the work environment became too toxic, and then temped, and decided to start my own business. I was in the transition between temping and starting my own business when his job started to fall apart.

His job had become more stressful when he was promoted to a position that was created just for him. Thing was, this job didn't have any sort of job description, so he was unsure of what he was supposed to do. The underwriters he worked under all had different ways of doing things, and each of them expected him to conform to her method and no others. He kept getting his work sent back to him because he'd done it one way, and they wanted it another. He'd do it that way, and then someone else would send it back. It was quite frustrating for him, and he didn't deal well with the stress of performing poorly. He was a perfectionist who was being told he couldn't meet standards, and it was because the standards kept changing.

He started to disintegrate right in front of me. He used me as an excuse, partly, said I was neglecting him, not giving him enough attention. I was trying to work on a graduate degree in my spare time, but because of the fibro, I was doing it online. He was in school too, trying to get his bachelor's finished. We were both working full time. We were busy, both of us.

And then it came down to this: I walked into the kitchen that morning in October 2002 and found him standing in the kitchen with a knife, with blood dripping off his arm. We'd been married five years, and I knew that our lives would never be the same. I took him to the hospital. He met with a social worker. Then I dropped him off at home, which was now the apartment, made him promise he'd be safe and not hurt himself again, and went to the temp job I was to start that very day. I had to. I needed the work, which loosely translates means I needed the money. It got worse, as these things tend to do.

CHAPTER 2

After the blood-dripping-down-the-arm incident, Stew went to outpatient treatment, which meant he had to be at the hospital every day. No work for six weeks. I tried to support him, both emotionally and financially. And I had my hands full. I was in grad school, too. Eventually I had to give up on that idea. I couldn't do it all, after all. I couldn't even do a part of it some days. But it was hard to let go. I'd dreamed of continuing my education for years. I thought I could do more than what I'd been doing. I had aspirations that exceeded my abilities. It was hard for me to give up. It left a hole in me, and I never made a serious attempt to get back to it. I'd learned my lesson.

After outpatient treatment, Stew attempted to go back to work, and it worked for a short while. For a company that was primarily health care focused, his employers were terribly unconcerned with his illness. Mental illness isn't given the same degree of respect as physical ailments, and it frightens us in a way other chronic conditions don't. If it could happen to likable Stew, who had seemed okay before, it could happen to anyone. His work environment was difficult. People gave him contradictory messages, day after day, about how he was to do his job. One manager would want things one way, another a different way, and the confusion made him angry. No matter what he did, he felt as if he couldn't do it right. They liked him just fine, when he was normal Stew. When he became mentally-ill Stew they took a step back, as if he were contagious. He was confused, frustrated, and he didn't know what to do.

Stew eventually became fixated on his "evil" co-workers, though I never had any illusions that anyone cared about him or what might happen to us, not after the first time I went to see his boss, to tell him Stew was in the hospital. The response was essentially, "Yeah, well, good luck with that." He actually took two steps back from me while I was talking to him, two steps back and a twist of his body so he could run away with a wave and a "keep in touch." I might as well have told him his valued employee had turned out to be a serial killer. On the other hand, I don't regard them as evil. Just uncaring. Just...uninformed. Not interested. Like many people, they don't know what to do or say when things like this happen. Do they think it's contagious? Do they think it only happens to certain people? Do they understand how fragile the human mind is? Any human mind? Do they hope to avoid that knowledge by avoiding the evidence? Maybe. I don't know. I like to think they're just ignorant.

To Stew, his co-workers' lack of sympathy was devastating. He'd cared deeply for them, and he'd always been supportive when they'd needed something. It was his first real job, he'd thought he'd found his tribe, he'd worked there for three years. He thought those people were his friends, and when he discovered the truth — that the workplace is not a place for friendship — it was very hurtful. He felt shunned. They were scared of him, and that made him sad.

———

Stew's Last Job
By Stew

I struggled with the descriptions of my former boss and former co-workers at my former place of employment, hereinafter referred to as Subsidiary of Big Health Insurer. I didn't want to carry my grudge too far and be too empathic about things. But I can only sum up these people honestly in one way: the embodiment of evil. I don't say that lightly. These are some of the most crass, calculating, unfeeling, resentment-filled, unforgiving, soulless people I've ever had the misfortune of meeting. And to think for three years I considered most of them "friends." My true friends have never bitten me in the butt as much as these knuckle-draggers have. And the former boss is the worst of the bunch.

My story at Subsidiary of Big Health Insurer goes back a while. I started at the Subsidiary as a temp worker, filling in for an underwriter when she was on vacation for two weeks. I admit, the first day I walked into the office it felt like a comfortable fit. Everybody was friendly, including the person who was teaching me. It was a fun two-week assignment, and the head of the underwriting department told me to keep in touch. He liked the job I did, and he liked the way I interacted with his people.

A few weeks later, I had another temp job with another department at the Big Health Insurer. I made sure I said hi to the gang at the Subsidiary, and boss told me that an underwriting assistant job opening was coming up and that I should stay close and apply.

Well, as events happened, I got the job, and soon established my territory as one of the fastest underwriting assistants that the department had. (Actually, after about a year and a half of being there I learned how to calculate my results, and was doing one and a half times the volume of work of one co-worker, and about twice the volume of work as another.) My reward for doing such good quality work quickly was to be promoted to financial underwriter, a brand-new position.

Unfortunately this is where things start to crumble. I was promoted faster than either of my co-workers. One had two years more experience, another had about a year more experience. I was also promoted faster than anybody in the operations section (which was a terrain ruled by one of the coldest people in Seattle.) So while publicly people applauded me on the promotion, secretly they resented it. I must interject here that the Subsidiary was a company of twenty-five people: twenty women and five men. All the men — save for myself and one male in operations — were management level.

This financial underwriter position was a newly formed position. In an industry that lives and dies by regulations, this was the kiss of death. This newly formed position had with it no set of procedures or guidelines that one could follow. One was at the whim of one's superiors when it came to figuring out what one was to be doing at any given time. One of my tasks was to help out the other underwriters in, well, underwriting. Every year, existing polices needed to be renewed but an underwriter had to figure out whether that policy could be renewed at the current rate, or if incidents had happened over the year that would force that rate up or down. One of my assignments was to do this underwriting process for policies in eastern Washington.

This should have been a relatively mundane day-to-day task that I could get help with from any of the other three underwriters. After all, one had just celebrated her twentieth anniversary with Subsidiary, another had been with the company fifteen years, and another had been there for ten years. Forty-five years of combined experience should have been a reasonable amount of resources for me to plug into.

Wrong.

Because they each had their own way of doing things. You'd think Underwriter 1, having been there for twenty years, would have had a set of procedures for doing renewals of existing business. After all, I had just finished compiling a list of procedures for the underwriting assistants, a task that received high marks from my boss, and my boss' boss. But nope. Twenty years at the Subsidary and a procedures manual for doing renewals had not been developed.

Which would have been fine and dandy, I probably could have split the difference, had Underwriter 2 shown me exactly how she did things. (After all, it was primarily her load I was helping with by doing eastern Washington). And I did. She sat down with me for hours at a time, showing me which buttons to push, and how to calculate experience-rated renewals for group life insurance premiums. She showed me how to program the database which enabled me to pull reports based on all types of criteria. She gave me a wealth of data. And it was all for naught.

Because, what she neglected to tell me, is that no matter how I did my job, if the forms weren't correctly filled out when given to Operations, it was kicked back to me to fix.

Which again, doesn't sound like that big of a deal. To which, I reply: There was no set standard for how the form was to be sent to Operations. Any one of nine different people would receive my form with the renewal information (People, let me clarify: Four of them were women over sixty, three of them were women over forty, one was a woman in her thirties, and one was a guy in his twenties. [I don't want to sound ageist or sexist, but most of these people were set in their ways and they weren't going to change anything. These were women who, when we received new computers, were scared shitless for days because their desktop environment had changed. It's the first time I ever heard of a department collectively complaining because their computers were faster]).

There were (at least) nine different ways to fill out the forms. I just had to figure out which person wanted which format (which felt like it rotated on a daily basis.) Again, I was out of luck because there was no standardized set of procedures. I even discussed the dilemma with the Head of Operations, and she proceeded to tell me to "just get it right." It became so agonizing that I was given one form back with a sticky note telling me "Everything was correct, but everything needs to be in all caps." When I became frustrated with that, I walked over to another person and asked her if she wanted it in all caps and she replied, "We never do it in all caps. That just looks ugly."

So more and more of my work was returned to me, which affected our team turn-around goals. (If the team made its goals each month for all months in a quarter, everybody on the team earned a half-day off. If the team made all four quarters it got an additional half-day off, for a total of three free days off per year.) By now my boss pulled me aside and said, "You gotta get those forms done correctly and on time, or you're going to cost the team its days off." When I explained the situation to him, he nodded and said, "I understand. These women aren't always reasonable. But you gotta play by their rules." So I said I'd do my best and sauntered off to do my job.

But the forms kept coming back to me, and more complaints were lodged with the boss. And this is where I fault the boss: He did nothing to stick up for me. He let the Operations manager and the Operations team browbeat him into me taking the whole blame for the team losing their precious days off.

But that's not what made the whole department evil. It gets worse from there.

It was customary to give cards on people's birthdays. Typical office stuff. It was common for those who were closer to give cards on other special occasions — anniversaries, baby showers, wedding showers, etc. We'd pass around the hat and take up donations for co-workers' babies, then the office secretary would run down to Babies'R'Us and buy a gift certificate. We had one lady who suffered from cancer and a donation was taken to buy her flowers or some other trinket for her hospital room. It was that kind of office.

Or so I thought.

When C was out of work for a month with cancer, the company sent a Get Well card to her, plus many individuals (including me) sent her cards. Some of the girls even called her up one day when she got home from the hospital to wish her well.

M's seventeen-year-old son was shot and killed at a party one tragic May night. The entire office went to the funeral. A condolence card was signed by each staff member. I sent another card on my own volition, and emailed M a couple of times after she came back to work to make sure she was okay. I even got into an online argument with a guy about gun control when she asked me to, because she knew I was a good debater.

Even J, one of the newest sales people, was thrown a party and received a $75 gift certificate when his son was born.

I was in the hospital on two occasions, both times for over twenty days. I received not a single card. I received not a single phone call telling me to get better. I received not a single email from anybody telling me I could talk to them.

My boss, the guy who wanted me to work for him, made absolutely no effort to reach out in my time of need.

Co-worker 1, the person who I laughed and cried with the most while during my stay at the Subsidiary, didn't send me a single email. Didn't call me. Didn't lift a finger to see if I was okay.

Co-worker 2, a self-professed Christian who was the first with the birthday cards to even the people she didn't care for, didn't even acknowledge MY emails to her.

Co-worker 3? I mourned the loss of her son with her. I made her laugh at my silly jokes. I understood her frustrations with the sales force. I even chatted with her about therapy. She made not a move to console me when I lost my mind.

I think I understood Co-worker 4 better than most people. I was often the first person she would come see when she was having computer problems. She shunned me with silence.

These are the evilest people I have ever known. I wrote them all an email around the holidays, after I got out of the hospital the second time.

Hi there...

As some of you may know, November 13th is my termination date.

I just have one question for most of you: Why didn't anybody ever call to check up on me? Send me a card telling me to get better? Even a simple email saying that I was thought of?

I put in what I thought were three quality years there with y'all. I thought I was liked and respected. But I know now that I wasn't.

For those of you who don't know what happened to me, I'll tell you.

On May 28th, I woke up with severe stomach pain. The pain was so bad that had Monique not stopped me, I would have taken a whole bottle of pills (I don't even know what I grabbed) and I was going to wash it down with a bottle of wine... I wanted to die.

I went to the ER, where I was diagnosed with a peptic ulcer and major depression, with suicidal thoughts. I was admitted into the Steven's Hospital psychiatric care unit.

I spent a month there in intensive group therapy. During this time, it was on an almost-daily basis that I would wake up with severe images in my head, and I would grab a knife and slice on myself. Sometimes I would wake up with thoughts of filleting myself and frying up and eating my own flesh. I became obsessed with the thoughts of hurting and maiming myself. Over the past six months I've probably cut myself, on purpose, over one hundred times. I've scratched myself with my own thumbnail to the point of leaving scars. I've tried to strangle myself, and I've done some nerve damage to my fists for punching things.

So after that month in the hospital I got to see a therapist twice a week, a psychiatrist once a month, and group therapy once a week.

I now have $15,000 in hospital bills, because (health insurer/employer) has screwed up on handling my claims. I've burned through my twenty psych visits per year pretty darn quickly, so I'm out over $300 a month for medical care. I'm on eight different medications just so I can halfway function in society without harming myself or others. I still have visions, and I still cut myself occasionally. But get me around a group of people and I tend to get a bit psychotic.

I've been diagnosed with major depression, anxiety, paranoia, borderline personality disorder, moderate psychosis, with a hint of schizophrenia. I take meds to help me sleep at night and meds to help me wake up in the morning.

And here's the greatest part of it all: Because I'm so unpredictable day-by-day (sometimes hour-by-hour) my wife has left. I can't really blame her.

So now I have to move into a one-bedroom apartment. My friends that I can trust have moved out of the Seattle area to look for work elsewhere. My family is trying to be supportive, and they do their best, but they're seven hundred miles away.

And you know what hurts the most? The thing that hurts more than taking a knife and cutting chunks of my arm? The fact that none of you ever took a moment to ask me how I was.

The fact that I was ignored — even when I (and Monique) tried to contact a few people — sliced through me. People I thought were reliable, people that I thought I could count on, people that I took time out to ask how they were doing when they were in the midst of their own hell...didn't even have a minute to ask me how I was doing.

What did I do to any of you to deserve that?

I know each of you have a story that you can tell that rivals mine...we all go through our own personal hell at one time or another...and there's no way that mine is of any significance to what any of you have/had/or are going through. But...at least if I knew about it, I hope I remembered to sign the card that was passed around, sent you a quick email asking how things were going, gave you an extra smile in the file room, did something to show that I was at least human enough to care.

I'm more disgusted with myself even thinking that people at [Subsidiary] care. "We're here...we're with you": Bunch of bull.

I can't honestly wish that any of you have a happy holiday season. The best I can do is I hope none of you have a tragic holiday season...

Stew

And you know what I got from writing that? I'll tell you what I got. I got a call from the sheriff's office and a frantic call from my psychiatrist making sure I was okay. Even when I reach out to slap them upside the head, I get smashed back, thinking that I was doing something wrong.

So, that about sums up the last job I ever had. Names, of course, have been changed to protect the guilty.

———

I don't believe in evil, not like Stew did. His former co-workers weren't evil, they were just self-centered and ignorant, or else they just didn't care. I'm not sure. But they're just people, and sometimes people let us down. Sometimes people aren't everything we'd hoped. There are times when we're all on our own — each of us — and this was one of those times. Things happen. But for Stew, it was such a harsh judgment, and another thing he couldn't let go of. It ate at him, like a cancer.

His last job lasted a year from the time of his first cutting. He persisted in trying to return to work, but it didn't work out. His illness was getting the upper hand. Eventually they let him go, put him on disability, and that was it.

He stayed at home and he went to therapy and he worked on getting better, and the doctors worked on fixing him. He said he'd help out with the bookkeeping business I'd started, and I sincerely hoped he could, because my income and his disability were all we had, and the disability wouldn't last.

And one day Stew snapped again. It's hard for me to talk about the details. The psychotic break that accompanied this episode caught me off guard. He accused me of being against him. He went into his own little world, where reality took on a whole new dimension. I didn't know where Stew had gone, but he was most certainly not present as he had been before, when he was just slightly nutso, when he was just unable to cope. Now he was psychotic.

It started when one day I came home and he was gone. He called and said he'd had to go to the ER, that there was something wrong, and he couldn't say what it was, but he was sorry. So I looked at his computer and I found emails from the new love of his life, the one who understood him, he had told the new woman, like his wife couldn't. I was sad but mostly I was angry.

He was ill, and I knew that, and he was no longer employed. For months, while he'd been on disability, unable to return to work, I'd taken care of both of us. The things that were too difficult for him, paying bills, shopping — making sure Things Got Done — I did, and I dropped out of grad school, and he'd said he'd help me with my business, so he sat at his computer while I was out working and he developed emotional attachments to other women, and that was his contribution.

I drove to the ER, where I found him clawing at his leg and making it bleed, waiting for a doctor to talk to him. I was so disappointed in what had happened to us. I had once thought I could count on him, and now I knew I could no longer count on him at all, that I was alone and yet, still, I had to take care of him, for he was like a child, or an adolescent, all caught up in what was going on with him, and there was no one else.

And he did not know me, except as the embodiment of evil who was trying to keep him from the woman he loved. Or the women he loved. He was not particularly good at differentiating among them by this time. After his problems started, he'd developed a habit of coming home and crying because (insert name here, it varies) didn't love him back, and how could he ever hope to get over her? As the patient wife who knew her husband was having serious emotional and mental problems, I tried to be helpful, but really, being shoved aside like that did not go over well with me.

We drove home from the ER separately, once he'd been seen by the social worker and had promised not to harm himself. I talked to his mom on my cell phone on the way home, and I cried, because he didn't even like me anymore, and I didn't know what had happened to us. I sobbed pitifully, and I knew that this was what I deserved, for having left my first husband.

Eventually, Stew and I worked on establishing a truce, in between recriminations and fighting. He said I neglected him. I said he was selfish. Among other things that were said.

I'd thought he was the one person who would not let me down. As a result, it took me a long time to learn to trust again, certain as I've been that if it happened once, it can certainly happen again. And would. His first "affair" was with someone he'd met online, while he was at home supposedly helping me. Off on disability, he spent his days at the computer, but not, as he'd told me, doing what I'd asked or looking for options for his illness, but striking up friendships with lonely women.

And we broke up. I could not be married to someone who imagined himself in love with other women. He couldn't understand why I couldn't be more supportive. He needed someone to help him, advise him, comfort him, and why shouldn't it be his best friend, who just happened to be me? I was also the wife, but that distinction meant nothing to him, so it ceased to mean anything to me. It just couldn't be done. He was hurt when we "broke up," and he said I left him first, and it remained a matter of contention between us, with him insisting that he never acted on any of his feelings (other than professing his love to others and bad mouthing me), so we learned to just ignore it. For him, the fact that he hadn't had sex with anyone else was supposed to be enough, but for me, sex itself was meaningless.

He no longer had the emotional intelligence to make sense of it all. I believe this to be a borderline trait, as I've witnessed it elsewhere: The focus on oneself, with an inability to see anyone else as anything other than as a supporting player in one's own life story. I was supposed to understand how hurt he was that his feelings for other women weren't returned, and I was supposed to help him deal with that. For quite a long while, I didn't have the external resources to understand that not everyone saw the world this way. Subjected to this attitude day after day, I became certain that I was only a supporting player in even my own life.

Supporting players don't get the good parts. We're not even allowed to have feelings if they don't mesh with the star's feelings.

I couldn't take any more of it, and I began living my life as a separated individual

We bought a bed for the spare room, which had previously been filled with shelves and miscellanea, and we moved him in there, and I immediately started repairing my wounded psyche with sexual encounters, just so I could prove to myself that I wasn't a totally lost cause, that someone somewhere would still be interested in me. This was bad for Stew. He said I cheated on him, that this was the ultimate betrayal.

Diagnoses were made. Treatment options established. I kept working in order to support us, while feeling as if I were now the ultimate outsider. What did I matter anymore? I learned to cope. I felt lonely, I made some bad choices, I learned from my mistakes, I learned how to handle his crises, and I learned how to deal with nutso behavior. I learned how to comfort and soothe and be patient. I've never been very patient, so this was good experience for me. And I became the caretaker. There was no one else. His family was in California, too far away to see what he'd become, and often I thought that was for the best.

His mood shifts, for years, had been sudden and unexplainable. He was all over the map some days, from exultation to severe despair, and I had no hope of keeping up without putting my own health at risk. 2003 is mostly a blur. 2002? What was 2002? Was it a year? Where was I in 2002? I couldn't tell you. Perpetually off-balance, the search for equilibrium gave me no time to do anything but survive, and hide. I was ashamed, partly, and I felt alone. And yet I remember we laughed a lot. We made fun of things. We looked for stupid stuff to laugh at. That was part of survival too. We were in it together, after all.

At some point, we conceived the idea of writing a book together about our experience. I'm not sure this is that book, but it is a book nonetheless. Some of what Stew wrote for that book is included here, because this is in some ways his book too.

But it's also my book, not only because I'm the one here to tell the story, but because those who love a mentally ill person have a story too. They must learn how to manage without abandoning themselves. I did, for awhile. Part of me became lost in 2003. My attempts to keep Stew safe resulted in my own breakdown. I had the entire world to take care of on my own, and it became too much. One day I couldn't stop crying. I couldn't cope.

Yet I refused to abandon him, and some people could not understand that. But how could I leave someone to drown? He'd talk about ending up on the streets, another homeless crazy person, and I told him that was not going to happen. And it didn't.

————

Another Introduction
By Stew

Welcome to my world. In these pages you will learn more than you ever wanted to know about several different mental illnesses. I've been diagnosed with major depression, severe anxiety, manic depression, and borderline personality disorder (BPD). Though it hasn't been officially diagnosed, it has been suggested that I might also suffer schizo-affective disorder. And although nobody has suggested or diagnosed it, I suffer many of the same symptoms that a schizophrenic suffers. But, I must implore you, do not self-diagnose. It is imperative that you listen to what the doctors and experts have told you. The treatment regimen I'm on is for what I've been diagnosed with. I would never start a treatment regimen for an illness that I think I have, only for something that has been diagnosed by a doctor.

That, in and of itself, can be tricky. Since October of 2001 until today, I've had three MDs, two PhDs, two MSWs [Master's in Social Work], and three ARNPs [Advanced Registered Nurse Practitioner] treat me. I'm one of the lucky ones, where most of the ten have agreed with the diagnoses. One of the ARNPs suggested I was something other than borderline, but I decided to go with the odds and listen to the nine that seemed to agree.

But like I said, I was lucky. In some cases, borderline is not as easily identified as it was in mine. In some cases, borderline is a "catch all" bucket that all types of personality disorders are dumped into. The DSM-IV recognizes eleven separate personality disorders.

Paranoid
Schizoid
Schizotypal
Antisocial
Borderline
Histrionic
Narcissistic
Avoidant
Dependent
Obsessive Compulsive, and
Personality Disorders, Not Otherwise Specified

Some psychiatrists (though fewer and fewer) do not recognize borderline personality disorder as a true diagnosis. They feel the diagnosis is a "cop-out" and that more and different kinds of testing need to be used to further determine what is wrong with the patient. This flies in the face of conventional psychiatry, as borderline personality disorder was first listed as a full-fledged diagnosis in the DSM-III, which was published in 1980.

Just what is borderline personality disorder? I've been told many things about it. One psychiatrist told me that it was being on the border between neurosis and psychosis. Okay, what does that mean? Remember the TV show "Mad about You," which starred Paul Reiser and Helen Hunt? Everybody would agree that the characters played by Reiser and Hunt were neurotic; they tended to do things in a somewhat unconventional way. But they did things, and got their jobs done, and were able to have functional relationships with each other and with other people.

Psychotics tend to do things in an unconventional way, but don't get things done. There's a break from reality. And relationships with other people are not at all functional. Thus, the borderline bounces back and forth from being functional to being dysfunctional. The psychosis isn't full blown; they can identify what is real and what isn't. But they may choose not to. At least that's one explanation.

Another doctor told me that the phrase "borderline" was quite the misnomer because borderline personality disorder wasn't actually on the border of anything. He suggested generalized personality disorder would be a more appropriate, and possibly more useful, name for the disorder, as it was characterized by the general nature of symptoms.

Just what are those symptoms? The DSM-IV[1] says: "Individuals with borderline personality disorder show a generalized pattern of instability in interpersonal relationships, self-image, observable emotions, and significant impulsiveness. This pattern begins by early adulthood, occurs in various contexts, and is indicated when a patient meets at least five" [of the nine criteria.]

The incidents that Monique and I will relate to you here will show you how the borderline personality disorder manifested itself in my case. I just briefly want to go through the nine criteria, and underline which criteria I clearly met and others, maybe.

---

[1] Diagnostic and Statistical Manual IV, American Psychiatric Association, 1994. (Text from pdf.uhc.edu/what.php).

1. Frantic efforts (excluding suicidal or self-inflicted cuts or burns) to avoid real or imagined abandonment.

I think Monique can answer this one more objectively and subjectively better than I can. There are still times today that I feel she may "abandon" me. And I can get very clingy to avoid those types of situations.

2. A pattern of intense and unstable interpersonal relationships that may quickly alternate between extremes of idealization (the other person may be "put on a pedestal") and devaluation (the other person's negative qualities are now exaggerated.)

Good Lord, do I know this one all too well. Putting people on pedestals is what eventually led to the collapse of my marriage. Women A to Z, the names aren't relevant. Each of these I put on a pedestal higher than I put my own wife. But as soon as these people did something "wrong" (and they never knew they were doing anything wrong), I would devalue the relationship to nothingness. It's a wonder that any of these women still consider me a "friend."

3. Identity disturbance: sudden and dramatic shifts in self-image in terms of shifting values (e.g., sexual identity, types of friends) and vocational goals.

This one may not be as applicable to me, as described, but I do have trouble identifying who I am. I think in one of the later passages I describe how when I was a kid, sometimes I'd stare into the mirror and look at myself and lose track of who I was. I'd have to repeat my name, address, and phone number, over and over again, to myself, to "remember" who I was. Even to this day, I don't have a strong sense of who *I* am.

4. Impulsiveness in at least two areas that are potentially harmful (e.g., spending, sex, substance abuse, reckless driving, binge eating, excluding suicidal or self-mutilating behavior.)

There's no question I'm an impulsive eater. I can't say I'm an impulsive shopper because I never had much money to go shopping with, except to buy food. I would be impulsive with sex had there been a willing partner around. So I gave in to masturbation and masturbatory fantasies.

5. Repeated suicidal behavior or threats, or self-inflicted cuts or burns (e.g., self-mutilating behavior.)

That's me. I'm a cutter. Can't count the number of times I've cut. I used to do it batches of thirteen, now I'm down to eleven. Usually a little ritual involving sterilizing the knife, and then I'd bounce it on my arm a half-dozen times, and then slice: Six on one arm, five on the other. If it was really bad, I'd cut the top of my right hand (which is weird since I'm right-handed.) Then I'd wrap my bloody arms up in towels and call Monique to let her know what I'd done.

6. Significant, sudden changes in mood and observable emotion (e.g., intense periodic sadness, irritability, or anxiety, usually lasting a few hours and rarely lasting more than a few days; extreme reactivity to interpersonal stresses.)

At the worst of it, my moods could change quickly. I'd be as happy as clam shit one moment, and then have inconsolable sobbing the next. I could be joking and laughing about something, and then suddenly turn and be an anxious wreck. I imagine it wasn't fun being around me in those days.

7. Chronic feelings of emptiness; may be easily bored.

Emptiness I know well. I still experience that on most days. I think it's why I eat so much. I'm trying to use anything I can to fill up that pit that resides in me. I feel very much the hollow man most days.

8. Inappropriate, intense anger or difficulty controlling anger (e.g., frequent displays of temper, constant anger, recurrent physical fights.)

The rage in me seems to have subsided quite a bit. We'll see how it goes at the new gym. That's when I felt a lot of it before. Or, the gym was where I released a lot of anger. Not *at* anybody, but I bruised and battered my hand on the punching bag quite a bit because of the rage I was feeling. I don't notice it much anymore. Except when I see John Kerry bumper stickers.

9. Temporary, stress-related psychosis (symptoms such as paranoia or grossly distorted body image.)

I think I still go through this. Once, Monique and I went to a concert with bagpipes and drums (this was before I was diagnosed) and the banging of the drums and the playing of the pipes and the general commotion of the audience sent me over the edge. I wanted to run down to the stage and stop them from playing. I wanted to rip my skin off. I wanted to puncture my ears with needles so I couldn't hear anything. I was a wreck. I'm still that way with loud noises (and in my space, noise equals stress.)

So that, in a nutshell, is borderline personality disorder. In the next pages you'll be introduced to the cast of characters that have made up my life over the past few years. And you'll read about the personal struggles of a person who had to deal with me...as well as reading about the demons that haunted and still haunt me.

Stew's Cast of Characters

I feel obligated to present to you the crop of characters that have defined my life in the past couple of years. Being borderline, I have a hard time identifying who I am without relating it to other people. That's one of the big disturbances with the BPD person: they have very little sense of self. (Yet sometimes they have tremendous egos. It's one of the paradoxes that you see so commonly in BPD and especially in my life.)

Here they are, in no particular order:

Monique Colver, best friend and ex-wife. Also former primary caregiver. She's been through it all, including her own bouts with depression. If it weren't for Monique, I'd probably be dead. Her story coincides with mine quite a bit, which is why she's the co-author of this book.

Roberta Young, my mom. One of the two parental units in our story. Quite possibly the most supportive mom in the world, even if she doesn't understand everything that's gone on with me. Not once did I ever blame what was wrong with me on her (or my dad.) However, I imagine the past few years have had tremendous impact on them.

Kenneth Young, my dad. The other parental unit. I'm a lot like my dad in some ways, completely the opposite in others. In my family, emotions were something we tended to avoid. "Don't cry. Crying doesn't solve anything," was what I routinely heard when I found myself upset. And on a logical level, it's true. Crying doesn't solve anything. But I've learned to enjoy the cathartic release of a good cry.

There's only one thing I could "blame" on my father and that is that I learned from him to keep emotions held in. Holding in emotions worked for my dad, worked for his father, I think it worked for his brothers. It doesn't work for me, which is fine. I just wish I'd learned this fifteen years ago. However, my dad and I enjoy the search for knowledge. He has gone to great lengths, learning everything he can about BPD, other mental illnesses, the meds I'm on, and the various therapies I've gone through. This means, to me, he definitely wants to figure out a way to help me.

Jake Johnson, friend. Well, more than just a friend, he's the best friend a guy could ask for. He's an inspiration, a motivator, and somebody who will help with anything if you just ask. Jake and I go back to high school days, though we didn't really meet until a few years later. Jake and a couple of his friends were long-haired, heavy-metal listening, Big-Gulp-swilling, hot dog chompin' ruffians who caused trouble during lunch period at Yuba City High School. Jake and his miscreant buddies used a tennis ball to terrorize people walking down the hall. Usually, they'd just play catch, but when a "lesser" being got in the way, they'd bean the poor sucker with the tennis ball, in the back, or the head, or the leg. Needless to say, I got beaned a couple times.

It wasn't until three or four years later that Jake and I hit it off, when I ran into him at a mutual friend's place, where we'd gathered to play Dungeons and Dragons. Pretty soon we were terrorizing the denizens of Yuba City, Marysville, and Beale AFB. About two years into our friendship, we made the famous Pepsi Run: Yuba City, California to Denver, Colorado and back in sixty-nine hours, just to get several cases of Crystal Pepsi, an event we like to reminisce about almost every time somebody will give us a minute to talk about it.

Jake is a respectable member of society now, with a BA in English and a Master's degree in something I can never remember. But it's impressive when he says it, and he works for the State of California Finance Department in the IT section. He also has a black belt in Tae Kwon Do. Oh, did I mention he's legally blind? Like I said, an inspiration.

Dr. Richard Geiger, former therapist, back in my Washington days. I had more luck with Dr. Geiger than I've had with any therapist. I believe he was practicing Cognitive Behavioral Therapy (CBT) with me. As I understand it, with CBT the patient is supposed to learn what he is thinking about, and then interrupt that pattern of thought with a healthier pattern.

For example, when I'm anxious I usually let the anxiety overtake me. I have all the usual symptoms: rapid heart rate, shallow breathing, becoming more alert, adrenaline kicking in, etc. CBT is supposed to teach me to become aware of the fact that I'm feeling anxious, and then look at why I'm anxious, then to calm down, to put into practice the coping skills I've learned.

There are a few: Take a clonazepam (aka Klonopin), play a video game, take a hot shower, etc. Rather than give in to the panic and be completely unproductive, I'm supposed to take inventory of what's going on and then try to move myself into a "self-soothing" mode.

Dr. Geiger is a wonderful therapist because, unlike some therapists, he interacts with me. With another therapist who shall remain nameless, I felt I was just talking to a wall ninety percent of the time. Dr. Geiger relates experiences that he's had in his life and parallels them with what I'm going through, making him (a) seem more human, and (b) giving me actual insight that a person that is going through some of the stuff I'm going through can get better and have a happy life.

Unnamed Person A, business owner. Person A is an interesting person, and has played an interesting role in my life. I've been attracted to Person A from the first day we met, which was when Monique and I were still working on the marriage and we were helping Person A secure a loan for her business. For two years, my head was filled with intense fantasies and desires for her, and my heart leapt every time I saw her smiling face. She knows of my affection for her, and she politely declined my "advances" toward her.

A new chapter in this relationship opened up recently, as we've been emailing each other about mindless (and some not-so-mindless) chitchat. We even saw a movie together, at her invitation, a few weeks back. I believe we are to remain friends, but I also believe she has some guiding light to give me on my path.

Unnamed Person B, friend and classmate. Well, she's not much of a friend anymore. Not that anything happened to end the friendship. We just don't communicate much anymore. I think the most I've heard from her in the past year are a few e-cards that she sent to everybody on her email list. But that's okay. Person B was there for me when few others were. I thought I had a good group of friends that I could count on when I was in school and first hospitalized, but I didn't. And one day, when I was at school and was having a meltdown, Person B took me to the ER.

But there was a problem. I lusted after her the way I should have lusted after my wife. And when I was in the hospital I admitted that I thought I was falling in love with Person B, and that's just never a good thing to tell your wife. I never acted on my feelings for her, but we did go out for drinks a couple of times after class. She was a good friend when I needed one, but often the BPD mistakes "friendship" for much more.

Unnamed Person C, MSW and director of the day program at Stevens Hospital. Person C was a godsend in many ways. When I first went into the day program at Stevens Hospital, I was scared. Not only did I not know what was going on with my mind, my only experience with "mental hospitals" was "One Flew over the Cuckoo's Nest."

I was expecting stark white walls, stainless steel chairs and tables, white tile flooring, and therapists and doctors and nurses wearing white gowns or lab coats. Fortunately I was way off base. Person C was a bubbly person who was wearing regular clothes (I think slacks and a sweater.) The main room for the group therapy had bookcases with books, a TV and VCR, a coffee table in the middle with a half-completed jigsaw puzzle, a couch, a loveseat, two big comfy chairs, and a few other straight back padded, not-so-comfy chairs. There were windows letting in natural light on two of the walls (why did they have the crazy people on the ninth floor?) and the other wall had a white board for the therapist to write notes on. And the floor was covered with the industrial grade of carpeting that you see in office buildings and hospitals all over the place. But at least it wasn't hard tile. A lot of my fears vanished instantly when I saw that first group therapy room.

But it was Person C who helped a lot, which is also dangerous. Much like Person B, my feelings for Person C went beyond the professional level. Needless to say, she never did anything to encourage those feelings in me. I just assumed that if a person was helping me, she "liked" me. I experienced rejection when I tried to move in for a kiss, and she appeared to be genuinely frightened. That was not at all the reaction I was hoping for, let alone anticipated. Again, wanting the utmost in honesty, I told Monique what had happened. She probably should have shot me, because it wasn't the last time I would betray her.

Unnamed Therapist D. I started seeing Unnamed Therapist D right before my first visit to the day program, about two or three weeks before. I continued seeing her for about a year or so after that. She initially helped a little. I think anyone would have helped a little at that point. But the sessions quickly became nothing more than me rambling endlessly about something, and her nodding and saying, "And tell me more about that."

Then, in the last five minutes or so of our session I would stop talking, usually with a question that had just been asked, and I would stare at her blankly, waiting for her to give me some sound piece of advice that I could take and plug into my life and make it work better. Her sound pieces of advice were never quite what I was looking for. We always ended the session with, "Well, that's where we'll pick up next week," but the next week's session was never picked up there.

They were always started by me rambling about something that happened during the previous week. So we had a lot of unconcluded episodes. And of course, me being of weak character, I "fell" for her. She was cute, and she talked to me, so that of course meant there could be a romantic relationship, right? Who cared if she was married with kids? Who cared if she would jeopardize her practice? Bottom line was she seemed intrigued when I told her of the erotic dreams I had. Obviously we could act these dreams out, right? No. Of course not. Why did I even go there? Why did I tell her that watching her sit there in her chair was a turn on?

She said it was because I was missing something in my life. I wasn't having a "need fulfilled" so I was looking to get it fulfilled elsewhere. Of course my wife wasn't "fulfilling" my needs. My wants and desires were every place but at home. Who could blame Monique for feeling hurt?

Unnamed Person E, friend, kinda…sorta. For somebody who was three thousand miles away, Person E caused a lot of trouble in a short time. We met on (and this is the irony of ironies) a Christian web site. I'm not even sure what it was that we were talking about on the web site that caused us to start emailing each other, but we did. Our emails grew more and more friendly, and then more and more erotic. Then we started with the Instant Messenger, and we were chatting for a couple of hours several times a day. Chatting when I was supposed to be doing some stuff for Monique's business.

Eventually Monique figured out that something was up with Person E. Then she found some emails I wrote. A lot that happened in the immediate weeks after, I really don't remember. One could lay the blame at Person E's feet, but I don't. It was my fault. Obviously it was a path I wanted to go down, you can see that by reading the descriptions of the previous four people. But it's no shock that my marriage would come crashing to an end because of what I did or what I felt towards many of these other women. If it wasn't Person E it would have been somebody, sooner or later.

Margee Young Knapp Wall Ginter Thomas Foley, sister. My sister doesn't play a huge role in my life, other than being my sister. We're separated by eight years, three thousand miles, and one parental unit. Actually, we're more acquaintances that would kill for each other than anything else. My sister doesn't understand me or my problems, though I think she would like to. The problem is that I understand her and her problems all too well, and I think that scares her. She likes to keep people off balance so that she can be in control, but the fact is she's the one out of control…[redacted.]

If push came to shove, I'd have to say that I don't like my sister much. I wish I could say I have forgiven her for telling me that she wishes I had never been born (kind of a cruel thing to say to somebody, eh?) but I probably can't forgive her for that. Hell, on most days I agree with her, I wish I hadn't been born either, but to actually hear that from a sibling that you actually admired for a long time, well, that's pretty much just a gut-turning event that you don't get over very quickly.

If ever.

CHAPTER 3

So although Stew and I were no longer married in the conventional sense, we continued to live together, with him in the spare room. We tried to find equilibrium. I'd had to drop out of grad school shortly after Stew became ill. I suppose I had some resentment for that. He managed, despite his illness, to keep going to school, while I had to drop out because I had too much to do: Work, take care of him, support us. I lost a lot of time, I lost part of myself, I became nothing more than a means to an end. But I didn't know that yet.

We just lived day-to-day. It has been suggested to me that I should have left Stew, but the thought never occurred to me. We were still bonded in a way that wouldn't allow me to leave him to his own devices. He needed me, and I needed to take care of him. He was still my friend, even if I couldn't always understand what was going on in his head. I never considered leaving.

Being Sad
By Stew

I'm not sure if it was the first experience or not, but I remember when I was playing Little League (that would be about fourth grade or so) when I realized that people my age didn't get what I was saying some of the time.

I'd read a lot of Peanuts comics, and had quite the collection of Snoopy books. In one comic strip, Linus had a baseball mitt on his head, and Schroeder said something like, "Don't be such a clown, Linus, you'll never catch a ball that way." And then a ball proceeded to drop right into Linus's glove for a perfect catch.

One day in Little League practice, we were doing some catching drills. The kid in front of me had put his glove on top of his head *a la* Linus, and it reminded me of the comic strip. So I said, "Don't be such a clown, you'll never catch a ball, that way." And this kid proceeded to tear me up one side and down another, saying things like, "Oh, like you should be saying stuff. You dropped three balls in left field the other night." And, "You're such a worthless player, you can't catch anything." And more stuff along those lines. I began to tear up and went running to the parking lot, to my dad's car.

Soon the coach of the team came to talk to me, but I felt that I had already said enough, so I didn't explain it to him. I figured, why bother? Nobody would understand anyway. Besides, the kid was right, I pretty much was a useless baseball player.

———

Living with him was not easy.

Living with another person is hard enough, or can be. Living with someone who crushes on every other woman he meets when said person was, until recently, a devoted husband, is really hard. It's not that I was supremely devoted to being a wife anymore—his lack of interest in me killed that off. But I was eager to reestablish myself as more than a caretaker, as someone who provided but who wasn't at the top of his list. I dated randomly, my only motive being a sex life. I was certain that love and marriage were out of the question for me permanently. It wasn't worth the effort, it wasn't worth the heartache, and it would never end well.

In my lowest moments I considered it my penance for having left my husband of twenty years. What did I expect? A happily ever after?

One night I stayed out all night, and when I returned home in the morning Stew was distraught. He couldn't believe that I'd actually slept with another man, that I could betray him in that way. After all, as he said, "I never did anything about it," by which he meant acting on his feelings for his love interests.

I refrained from pointing out that this was likely due to the fact that his love interests were either 1) not interested or 2) thousands of miles away. That one issue remained a point of contention, and eventually we just didn't discuss it at all. Better to disagree and ignore it. He thought that my being physically unfaithful was the epitome of betrayal, while I thought it was falling in love with multiple other women.

It's not that difficult for a woman to get male attention when all she's looking for is casual sex, and it was one thing I could enjoy that didn't cost any money, of which I had none. But it made Stew so angry. An angry schizophrenic is not a happy schizophrenic. Well, a schizophrenic is not happy as it is, but my failure to mold my life around his illness, even while taking on the responsibility of meeting his daily living needs and making sure he got the medical care he needed — and being his friend, the one person he could tell anything to (and did) — wasn't enough. He wanted me faithful to the idea of the marriage we'd once had too.

Like, as if. I was far too angry at the sharp turn my life had taken. It was time for me to do what I wanted to do, now that I was no longer committed to anyone. At least, not committed in that couple sort of way. I hadn't been single since I was eighteen, and it was an experience I was determined to have, no matter the cost. My promiscuous ways didn't last long, but at the time I thought I didn't want any . . . entanglements. Girls just want to have fun, right?

After about six months of my working to keep us afloat while exploring my new single status, and Stew trying to acclimate himself to being mentally ill, and with us both exploring the options for his care while the doctors tried to find a combination of medications that would work for him, I realized we needed separate apartments, but close by each other. I needed my own separate life, my own separate space. I'd never had that. We looked in our same apartment complex, and when I walked into my potential new apartment I fell in love with it. It was on the second floor, a corner unit, and it had trees outside all the windows. It was like my own personal tree house and there was a deck for the dog, Honey, who'd replaced Jesse after we'd lost her. (Losing Jesse was another stressor for both of us, but especially Stew.) We found Stew a one bedroom lower-level apartment in a different area of the complex, close enough to walk back and forth, but far enough apart so we'd each have our own private space. We were truly happy to have our own spaces, and it was an ideal situation for both of us at the time. He could come to my apartment daily, but then he could go back to his, and we both felt relief. It made it easier for me to care for him, now that we could interact when we wanted to, not because we had to.

————

Stew's Diary Entries

May 15, 2003

Listen. Can't you hear that? Why is it that I'm the only one who can hear it? It's as clear as a bell in my head: Literally hundreds of voices all talking and clamoring for attention. Sometimes it all blends together into a mindless "whir" of white noise. When it's like that, it's not so troubling. It is times like now, when I can hear individual voices, that it bothers me. I think that's why I sometimes recite the same song lyric over and over again, to drown out the other noises. Right now Toby Keith's "Angry American" is going over and over again.

But the repetition of songs has always been there. I'd always get a tune stuck in my head and it'd stay there for weeks on end. In third or fourth grade, I had Bible school songs going on in my head. I'd have to think about it more to remember if I heard the voices as long ago as that. If I had to guess, I'd say yes. I remember feeling like I had voices and noise and clutter in my head for most of high school, and even junior high.

The voices don't say much. Yet it's enough to drive me crazy. Mostly it's highly critical stuff, and there are different voices. I hear my mom and dad, Dr. Hansen, Dr. Geiger, Nick, Jake, and Monique. Sometimes I hear voices from past teachers; sometimes I hear society's collective voice. At other times I hear what I believe to be God and Satan. Satan's voice is eerily similar to my own. God's voice is eerily similar to my own, too.

The voices were talking in the shower just now. They were saying how I should be writing, but there was another voice telling me how crappy a writer I am, and that I shouldn't even try. Another voice said I should just sit down and read the Bible. Often when I feel like I'm supposed to read the Bible, and don't, I feel guilty. I'm reading Numbers right now. Pretty interesting stuff, how each of the twelve tribes of Israel were to take a census of themselves.

Anyway, the voice that told me to write, well there were actually a number of them, won out tonight. I'm sitting here writing this…this dreck.

May 18, 2003

"Write about what you feel," people have told me for the past couple of years. Who cares what I feel? I don't feel anything most days. It's just sort of this numbness that feels as if it will last forever. Like being awake after being given anesthesia, the body and mind are numbed to any real stimuli, but the body can still move and function. And the mind wants to function. It really does, but it's like it's stuck in neutral.

Can you imagine a worse fate? Having a mind that is completely stuck in neutral for eternity, but having a body that could function if the mind would tell it to? And knowing that your mind is going to be forever stuck? Sometimes being self-aware is a painful proposition.

Right now I'm staring at the keyboard, wondering what my next thought should be, and it occurred to me there is no next thought. And that's the frustrating thing, knowing that there is no next thought. Sometimes I just realize that I'm thinking about nothing, so I ponder that. Is there a bigger waste of time than pondering your own sense of thinking about nothing? Yet, if I didn't ponder that, then I literally wouldn't be thinking of anything.

I thought a lot about cutting today. The only reason I didn't do any is because I spent most of the day playing baseball on the computer, or other distractions. I even looked at the knife briefly, and realized I was going to have to wash it, and burn it first before I did any cutting — it was last used to chop up a frozen pizza — can't go around getting pepperoni jizz in my wounds.

Sometimes I think it's weird that I don't have any piercings or tattoos. With as much as I like cutting or scratching myself, you'd think that I'd have a number of 'em. I think branding might be something that would be kind of cool. I've been thinking about getting a cigar, enjoying it, and then snuffing it out on my arm. I'm wondering how that would feel.

But branding seems like it would be an easy type of pain. It's over quickly. It seems like it would be done before the pain even registered. I wonder what kind of brand I should get. Something classy, not like a K-Mart or Target brand. The Pepsi logo would be appropriate. Yes, the Pepsi logo on my right bicep. That sounds like a good idea.

Is there much risk of infection with branding or burning? It's hot metal. Wouldn't the heat kill the germs? Rub on a little anti-bacterial ointment afterwards, and then a few days of Noxzema to soothe the burn, and it'd be good as new, wouldn't it?

I don't even feel guilty for thinking about this right now. I'm a little scared that I might actually try it, but really, don't I deserve it? Don't I deserve the pain I inflict on myself? I mean, I'm quite the sinner, and sins deserve to be punished, so isn't it better that I punish myself to get it done and over with? What's the point in waiting for something to come down and strike me? Why don't I just strike myself? It saves time and energy for everybody else who should be doing it. And since I wronged them in the first place, I might as well save them the time and money, right?

I just took my nightly pills. One lithium, one Geodon, one trazadone. Three little pills to make sure I don't go schizo in the morning. It's a bummer when I don't take those nightly pills. I end up not sleeping very well, and I'll wake up in a downer mood with a greater likelihood of having some type of psychotic break during the day. Taking all of these medications is like playing craps or roulette at the casino. It's not that anything I'm taking is going to cure anything, it's more like having something severe happening less frequently.

The Zoloft I take in the morning doesn't mean that I'm not going to be depressed during the day; it just decreases the likelihood that I'll slip into a major depressive episode. And for this run of luck, I pay $400 a month. Is that a good gamble? Would I be better off putting $400 on Black 13? If it came up, I'd be $14,000 richer. That would pay for a couple of years worth of meds AND therapy.

May 23, 2003

I'm kind of down right now. It's 10:30 at night, and the people in the apartment upstairs are having a party. It sounds like it, anyway. It's times like this, when there are muffled voices and music and stomping, that I can't tell where my thoughts end and the reality of their party begins. I don't really hear their music as much as I feel it vibrating through my being. I don't hear their voices as much as I hear mufflings that I confuse with the voices I already hear. It's times like this when the anxiety reaches a more frenzied state, and that cutting becomes a viable alternative.

I'm kicking myself for not being strong enough to go up there and ask them to turn it down a hair. I rationalize, "Oh, it'll probably be only a little while longer." Or, "It's so loud, they probably won't hear me knock." Or, "I'll be asleep in a few minutes anyway, so it's no skin off my nose." But the thumping of the bass and laughter is getting louder. It's rattling the fan above the stove. My head is thumping harder and harder.

And I wonder if it's jealousy. Maybe I'm jealous because I wasn't invited to the party. And if I was invited, I probably wouldn't go anyway because the noise and people would make me feel uncomfortable. Such a state of contradiction I live in.

How come people can't close doors softly? How come it must always be with a slam? How come it's always people upstairs who are the noisy ones? Why is it me who is always persecuted like this? Why am I feeling sorry for myself now?

It's so hard to concentrate with all of this noise, both real and imaginary. And to think there are some people who actually think I've accomplished a lot in my thirty-two years. What dunderheads. If only they knew how little I've actually done, they wouldn't be that amazed.

I didn't think the music could get any louder but it just has. If I were playing a stereo in my own apartment, I wouldn't be able to hear it this well. Sounds like about thirty people up there. And I know they have the same floor plan as mine, so I have no idea where they would put thirty people.

The anxiety has just crept past the boiling point. I'm going to go get my knife.

Seven new cuts, all on my left arm and hand this time.

I took the big knife this time, washed it in hot water and soap, used my lighter to heat the knife up, and then bounced the blade on the arm a couple of times…and then… slice. It's cool how the blood doesn't immediately appear. What's weird is that it hurt more today than it normally does. Usually I feel some type of sensation when I cut, not something I would describe as pain, but some type of sensation. This time it felt more like the skin was being ripped than cut. Probably time to sharpen my blades.

And wouldn't you know it, I was right. The party ended about five minutes after I cut. Talk about dunderheads.

May 28, 2003

For the past several days I've felt twitchy. My right hand keeps trembling, and at times I feel the trembling up into my elbow. My breath seems ragged, and my heart feels like it's pounding faster than normal. I've been trying to take my anti-anxiety pills when I notice this coming on, but it hasn't seemed to help much.

I just got up from a nap. Before getting up I had visions, though they weren't of cutting myself. They were of actually cutting something off. I thought and envisioned a number of different ways to cut off my middle finger on my left hand. I thought about using my cigar cutter, though it's over at Monique's place right now. And I thought about the couple of knives I have, and which one would be better for it — the Wilkinson self-sharpening carving knife, or the heavier and stronger butchering knife. It's a good-sized hunk of bone that I would have to chop through, and I'd really only get one good chance at it. Just hacking away at it seems like it would just take too much time and effort.

It's like that guy who was in the paper a few weeks ago, the hiker who got stuck underneath a boulder and he used his pocket knife to cut his arm off so that he could free himself. My arms are pretty thick. To use a pocket knife to do something like that seems very labor intensive. Not something I think I could do. But the finger, I think I could do.

But to what end? What would that accomplish? Would I be satisfied with just one finger, or would I continue to do it over the years and be left with a finger-less hand? That would sure decrease my typing speed a lot.

But why do I think about it? Why is it now almost a compulsion in me to have to find out what the consequences would be if I chopped off a finger? Why do I feel like it's the next logical step?

What am I feeling? I'm feeling scared. Of what? Of stuff. I was lying there in bed, and I thought, "I should read the Bible while I'm here and awake." But I didn't want to. And then I felt guilty. I feel like I'm not being as devout or as "good" as I should be when I don't cater to the religious whims that come over me. I feel as if I'm denying God. And the last thing I want to have happen is for God to deny me.

I took a look at the Books to Prisoners web site. Those people appear to have a completely different philosophy than I do. Sounds like they were amongst the protesters during the WTO riots a few years back. I just want to help get reading material to anyone who wants it, I don't want to get involved in an anti-establishment organization that sees big corporations and big money as evil. I like big corporations. Some of my oft-used items come from big corporations.

May 31, 2003

I saw something. Or at least I thought I saw something. Just now, while walking Honey Bear I turned a corner and jumped because I could've sworn there was somebody walking a dog just off to my left. But when I looked again, there was no one there. That's the second time today I felt and sensed and could've sworn I saw a presence that turned out not to be there. First time was also when I was out walking puppy dog, and I was sure there was somebody behind us. Frustrating feeling.

I've decided I want to become a criminal. After watching "Ocean's Eleven" and "The Italian Job," I've decided that I'm cut out to be some type of criminal. One thing about watching these shows, there's always at least one person who has some type of disability, like hearing loss. I'd love to see a movie where one of the members of the team has a mental disability, like bipolar disorder or schizophrenia.

How about a completely dysfunctional crew? You've got your bomb expert, he's deaf. A blind wheelman. "Lefty," the large one-armed "heavy." A safecracker with Parkinson's disease. And the ring leader is schizophrenic with visual and auditory hallucinations. Yeah, I think that'd work.

I was exploring the seedier side of the Web today, sites about hacking and cracking and phreaking. I also found sites that sell alternatives to marijuana, speed, and heroin. There was also this other site that had stuff for sale, from the basic lock picks to password generators to ways of making free cell phone calls.

I'm not sure what kind of crime I'd want to be involved in, though. Nothing where anybody got hurt. I don't know, a good heist of some type. But not gold. Gold is too heavy and too hard to deal with. Something like credit card fraud. Something where the only people who get really screwed are credit card companies and their insurance carriers. (Of course, the stockholders also end up getting screwed because it means a lower net income, blah blah blah.)

If I could figure out a way for 250,000 people to each send me a dollar, I'd do that. But sometimes you have to force them to give up that dollar, thus they get screwed by being investors in credit card and insurance companies. It all equals out in the wash.

Why should they get screwed? Why not? Somewhere along the way they've screwed somebody. We've all screwed and been screwed. Why not just profit from it once or twice?

And really, is getting caught that detrimental? Assuming I ever saw a prison cell, it would be a nice change, I think. Sitting in an eight-by-ten foot cell, staring at the walls. Not much different than my existence now. And there would be more people to talk to. Probably not the most pleasant of people, but it's not like the people I associate with now are all that great. Hmmm. Must ponder this some more.

And if I got away with it — say a score of $250,000 — then I wouldn't have to worry about much for awhile. I wouldn't have to borrow money from anybody. I could pay off my bills. I could give Monique some money. And then I could just hide away where nobody would find me. $250,000 minus $10,000 for bills, minus $40,000 to Monique, leaves me with $200,000. Invest in a fund that pays a 3% return annually = $6,000 a year. (Chart of financial returns goes here.)

Hmmm. Looks like I'd survive for ten years on that. I could live for sixteen years if I did $300,000. Or thirty-two years at $500,000. That would put me at sixty-four. Let's try $750,000. Seventy-eight years, I'd be 110.

What if I spent $50,000 a year? Okay, it looks like optimally I'd need to get a million dollars and spend $50,000 a year, and it would last me for about thirty years. If we assume that interest rates will rise during the next thirty years, we can figure that I'd get a consistent income for that thirty years, no problem.

But how to find a million dollars to steal? That's the difficult one that I will have to ponder.

June 5, 2003

I was fascinated with tattoos today. Driving back from Northgate I saw several tattoo shops, and I wondered how much it would cost to get one on my bicep. I think a ferocious grizzly bear would be kind of cool. But not knowing how much they cost, I had no idea if it was even a remote possibility. So of course I looked it up on the web. About $120 per hour, and small ones usually take about a half hour, so I imagine that the bear image that I'm thinking of would be about $200+ or so. No way can I justify that type of expenditure.

Then, after doing some more searching on the web, I found a list of what I would call post-op instructions relating to the care and management of a tattoo. What the hell is that about? I can't remember to take my meds three times a day, how in the world would I remember to apply moisturizing ointment on a tattoo SIX times a day for five days? I've seen people with tattoos, it seems that a lot of these people are lucky to remember to breathe, let alone care for a tat.

Ah well. There goes my fantasy of running cross country on a Harley with my bear tat waving in the sun. I don't know why, but I've been looking at motorcycles with keen interest, too. But I have such a lousy sense of balance that I also see myself splattered all over the ground after just hopping onto a motorcycle. It wouldn't even have to be running and I'd find a way to damage myself.

Over the past week or so, I've felt drawn to a lot of "macho" things. I purchased a new knife over the weekend, and I was fascinated by all the different blades. I've decided I want to start collecting knives as a hobby. I've always wanted a sword — I think there's something mystical about the Scottish claymore — a sword that was designed to take out the legs off oncoming horses during a battle. It didn't have to be very sharp, just basically a big piece of metal with a handle that the typical warrior couldn't really swing in battle. He'd grab hold of it, kneel down, and place it parallel to the ground, about knee high on a horse. When a horseman galloped up, the horse's legs hit the claymore and the steed went down, tossing its rider. The Scotsman then picked up his claymore and pummeled the rider, with garish results.

I've also been fascinated with guns again. I don't really want to own one, but I want to feel one in my hands. I want to fire one. I'm just craving the power that a gun gives somebody.

And cars. I've been reading *Car and Driver* recently, and have been interested in keeping up with the new trends in cars. I don't know why. Just again, I think I'm craving power.

———

By 2003, I was adjusting to life as a caretaker. Or trying to. But not living with Stew wasn't easy either. As much as this story is about Stew, it's also about me. It was almost too much for me, all of this, and I was subject to frequent bouts of depression. And I was tired. I didn't sleep well. I took to napping during the day, and often the urge overcame me when I was in my car, driving from one appointment to another, and I'd pull over and fall asleep. One day I went to get my hair cut by a client — she'd talked me into doing a trade, though I needed the money more than I needed my hair cut — but I was easily talked into things then. She charged me way too much for my hair, and I spent far too much time on her books without adequate compensation, and even during an appointment that I was paying for, she'd talk about her business. On this one day I got to her salon and I was so tired that I closed my eyes for a few minutes before I got out of the car.

It was a pleasant sunny day in Seattle and when I woke up it was an hour later. I woke up only because my phone rang, and it was a potential new client, so I drove away, without ever going inside the salon. Sleep mattered to me more, whenever I could manage it.

I often flaked out on people. I didn't have many friends in the area, hadn't had time to make friends since we'd been so busy dealing with Stew's issues, and I was convinced that socializing was not in my best interests. And I hate asking for help. Absolutely hate it. When I ask for help I'm fairly certain that people are judging me weak and incapable, and being judged is also not something I'm fond of. Any sign of weakness is to be avoided. I've always known that as long as I'm useful to people, things are fine. But as soon as I'm not — as soon as I'm the one who needs something — they'll want nothing to do with me. This may or may not be true, but what mattered is that it's something I'd always known as true.

So I broke down with the pressure of it all.

March 23, 2003
Journal Entry

It eats away at me, it threatens to devour me, it causes me to question everything around me. It makes me suspicious, and wary, and overly cautious.

I can't believe what I'm told, I can't believe who I am, because the doubt is strong, and inside of me it lies coiled, ready to strike at the slightest provocation, the merest hint, and when it does strike I can feel it down to my marrow, it's there, it's within me, and I don't know how to stop it, how to tame it, how to make myself listen to reason.

When the doubt is there, that's all I know. And I know, when the doubt is upon me, that I am unworthy, unlikeable, unlovable, an unpleasant blip on the radar, unnoticeable, and no matter the evidence, it is still what I know.

Rational thought goes out the window when the doubt comes in through the door, and it doesn't make any pretense of sneaking in, it doesn't have to, it barges in, it makes its way to me without hesitation, without its own doubt. It knows me, knows my weaknesses, knows how to get to me in the most effective, the most punishing, the worst ways. It is not difficult for the doubt.

I will, when the doubt is upon me, push away anyone who tries to get close because I know that in the end they will push me away, and the best defense is a strong offense. I will not let anyone in where I am safe in my knowledge of what I am not. "If only they really knew me," the doubt says, "they'd push me away even faster. They'd realize what I really am."

This self-defeating prophecy will come to pass if I am not careful. If I do not stop believing, somehow, that it is right and I am not, that I am everything the doubt tells me and not what I, or anyone else, tells me.

Why does it have so much power over me? I don't know. If I knew, if I knew the source of its power, perhaps I could eliminate it, or wear it down, or disregard its nagging voice. But I don't know. And so I think...if I don't know the source of its power, perhaps it is right, perhaps that's why it is so strong.

I don't know. How can I? Right now, all I know is doubt.

Later: I staved off the demons for another day. They almost had me, almost caught me in that death grip that feels like absolute utter despair. For a few moments, at least, they did have me there; for hours, at least, I held them at bay with all the strength I had. I've become stubborn though, perhaps it is age, perhaps it is just that I've grown tired of someone other than myself running my life. So I fight back, and I force them back into the dark places where they cower.

They cower because they are cowards, because they know that in the end I will win, and they will not, and because, in the end, they have no force strong enough to overcome me.

I just read a book Stew got for me about taming gremlins. It's a good book, it talks about reducing the attacks of gremlins to idle background chatter that we can be aware of but not put any credence in. We can hear our gremlins, take note of them, but we have the power to dispel their toxicity.

I'm working on it. Demons, gremlins, harbingers of doom and gloom — they tell me that what I was told growing up is still true. They reinforce negativity that has been in my life. They make me ashamed of who I am.

Rationally, I know the truth, but can any of us ever claim to be totally rational at all times? I'm a work in progress. I'll win, and they won't. It's as simple as that.

Turning Over a New Leaf
April 6, 2003
Journal Entry

So I say. A new leaf. Hmmph. Indeed. Why not? Another day, another leaf.

The dog did not want to cooperate this morning. Took her downstairs for her morning activity, the one she does upon first arising. That time of day, I'm barely coherent myself, and stumbling no less, so we just go to the bottom of the stairs for a few minutes while she takes the opportunity to relieve herself. Then we race back up the stairs so we can ponder the wisdom of climbing back into our respective beds (which may be the same bed, if she's in the mood) while we instead begin to work. I do, anyway, Dog is notorious for being a slacker.

Anyway, there we were at the bottom of the stairs. And she looked around.

She sniffed the grass, she looked underneath the stairs — certain there was a cat lurking about (she's been highly suspicious of cats ever since she found out there was one entering the premises while she was away) — then she turned her nose up in the air and looked off into the distance, as if the smell of a big juicy steak was in the air.

And she did not relieve herself.

I pulled her over to the ivy. That usually does it, the promise of soiling fresh green ivy, but not today. She just looked down at it, scoffed, and ambled alongside the border.

We moved back towards the stairs. Well, I moved back towards the stairs. She had no choice but to follow along. She looked under the stairs some more. She sniffed. She looked at sections of grass as if each inch were different and worthy of notice.

She did not relieve herself.

I entreated her to go about it, get it done, move on with it. I am notoriously impatient at that time of day. It's one of my character defects. She ignored me altogether. Sometimes I think she's part cat.

I gave up. I moved her towards the stairs and she moved up them, sluggishly, but up them all the same, which she wouldn't have if she did feel the need to relieve herself. Upstairs she asked to go back out onto her deck so she could go back to sleep. She'd slept there most of the night, after first falling asleep with me before deciding my snoring was too obnoxious.

And I sat down here to ponder the twelve million things I need to do before I see my first client in a few hours. Okay, perhaps that's an exaggeration. I am prone to exaggeration, to hyperbole, to overstatement, to histrionics. Not only prone, but addicted.

Back to my new leaf. I am, in addition to my penchant for drama, a serious overthinker. I think too much. I ponder. I think. I turn things over and over in my head until I've made a complete mush of it and don't know anything about it at all. I doubt. I am seriously thinking that people tolerate me. That in the overall scheme of things, I am unwanted, unlovable, unliked. I wish to turn over a new leaf and stop thinking this way. But what, I ask myself, if I'm RIGHT? Well, that just changes everything, doesn't it?

See what I mean? Too much thinking. Dog thinks too much too. Instead of just taking care of the matter at hand, she has to examine every blade of grass, every slight breeze, every motion within fifty yards to determine if it's worthy of notice. But then she forgets about it and does what's next on her agenda, and I'm certain that whatever she was just doing is gone from her mind altogether. This may be a function of being a dog with a short-term memory, or it may be a function of a devil-may-care attitude. I have no hope of being a dog, at least not in this life, but I could adopt her attitude.

I'll work on it. After all, what if people don't like me? Dog does. Well, when she feels like it. When she's up for it. When other pressing matters aren't intruding.

Sigh. I'm overthinking my DOG.

Will someone please stop me?

Later that day: This time I'll have to go to the ER, he says. I say no, I won't go, I won't, but there's nothing left of me. I am nothing, and there's nothing there, and the only people who want to be around me are those who I'm helping or who want something from me without being connected to me. No one wants to be connected to me because there's nothing there to be connected TO.

There's nothing left of me. I won't go, of course, though he says I have to, but I won't listen. There's nothing left of me, and there wasn't much to begin with, and now there's nothing at all. And it doesn't matter. There are no words of encouragement, blank endorsements, nothing. In the end, it's all the same. No one seeks me out.

And no, I'm not suicidal. I just want to not care anymore.

I'm empty.

There's nothing there.

Damn, I sound bad today.

I think I'll call my therapist, the one I can't afford. (And of course I didn't.)

Later, during the summer, I couldn't stop crying. I couldn't think straight. I could barely function. I felt alone, I was alone. I couldn't cope. I fell apart. I had to seek help.

And I recovered, and I started learning how to take care of myself first. It was not an easy thing tolearn, and it was not a quick process. But I had no choice. I knew that I had to help myself. Calling the crisis line was all well and good, but I was the one who had to do something, I was the one who had to get moving and change my perspective. It was up to me.

My first visit with the crisis intervention specialist went about as well as one could expect. I promised not to hurt myself. (Not intentionally, that is. Harming myself unintentionally is a fact of life because I'm clumsy.) I promised to follow up with my psychiatrist about my meds, to work at regaining my sanity. Stew wanted to help me, of course, but he was in his own private hell, and I felt as if there were no one I could call on. There was no one. Perhaps there was, but at the time all I knew was that it was up to me, and there was nothing anyone else could do. I had to keep working; I had to support myself, even with my concentration substandard and my motivation purely financial.

My psychiatrist/therapist — Stew's psychiatrist — said I was bipolar, and she prescribed combinations of different drugs. Later I found out I'd been overmedicated and misdiagnosed. It's no wonder I was a wreck, what with dealing with Stew and his issues and trying a cocktail of drugs that wasn't suitable for me, or my condition, which was simply depression. I don't mean that depression is simple, but it's certainly not bipolar, is it?

Stew and I remained fast friends through all of this. (Once I recovered from the shock of being rejected, anyway.) Someone asked me once if I felt like a martyr, and the thought had never occurred to me. It wasn't as if I was doing something I didn't want to do. The idea of leaving him to cope for himself was just totally foreign to me. He couldn't take care of himself, he had regressed chronologically, and he needed help. Who else was going to do it, if not me? And even if someone else would, could they do as good a job as I did? I didn't think so. No one knew him as well as I did.

Anyway, no one else offered.

CHAPTER 4

Mental illness is a funny thing. Stew began seeing shadows. He didn't know if it was because he has trouble with his eyes because of his meds, or if he was really seeing shadows. It made him a bit jumpy. And he claimed to communicate telepathically with the dog. I loved the dog, but we didn't communicate in that manner.

He had conversations with many people in his head. And yet, he was still one of the most perceptive and wisest people I'd ever met. He had a great mind, he was capable of much, even with the BPD and schizophrenia and anxiety and depression. And he was motivated too. I thought he'd be okay. Though I'd still be around to make sure.

We sat down daily and made a list of tasks for the following day. I'd email it to him, something concrete for him to follow through with and cross off. He continued his education, too. He even tested out of biology, meaning he didn't have to take it. He decided to try to test out of chemistry, too. He was smart.

———

Diary Entries
By Stew

November 18, 2003

Why am I so afraid of responsibility? I think about it, and I realize that most of the time, I feel that I'd rather end up homeless and on the street (actually, in my car) than in the vision of "success" that is talked about. There is something romantic to me about having a mattress in the back of my truck, and not having any worries about anything.

I even talked about this with my mom a few weeks ago, about how I'd survive if I was ever homeless. I've got the truck (actually SUV), the mattress, and other stuff I need to survive. I can put the rest of my belongings in storage (or give them to Monique.) I can pay $50 a month for a gym so that I have a place to shower, shit, and shave. And there are enough places out there that feed people that I'm sure I wouldn't starve to death. (When I was going to NAMI last year there was a guy who knew of five different shelters/churches that fed hungry people. He said he got a better variety of food being homeless than he ever did while he was working.) So I could exist without being a burden on anybody for a few hundred bucks a month.

Even in my early twenties, I saw something romantic about that. I chalked it up to wanderlust at that time, as I imagined myself wandering from city to city. My dad didn't understand that at all.

Once, when I was twenty, some friends from the Internet were planning to meet down in Hermosa Beach for a weekend. I packed a few things and headed down. First I stopped at my sister's in San Bernardino, and then I traversed the LA freeway system to the beach. There were about a dozen of us, and one of the guys let me crash on his couch. It was a trip of firsts for me — first time I was around pot smokers, first time I made a pass at a married woman, first time I took advantage of a woman while she was drunk/stoned.

I'll never forget. It was during the beginning of the first Gulf War, and it was about three in the morning and there were still about a half dozen of us at this guy's apartment, and suddenly the cops started banging on the door. The neighbors had complained because we had CNN up too loud. They weren't complaining three hours earlier when we had "The Rocky Horror Picture Show," on and ten of us were screaming the words to the movie at the top of our lungs. No, they called when we had quieted down and were watching the war.

Then, I wasn't ready to go home yet. So I drove across to Phoenix and met up with a lady I had been chatting with on the 'net. She and her husband had three daughters ranging from five to twenty-three. (I, of course, had a crush on the mom, and after I met the sixteen-year-old, I thought she was pretty hot, too.). Here this nice family, who had never met me before, put me up in the same house with their daughters. And I make a pass at the mom, rather forcefully, actually. (She also made the best chicken fried steak. Oh, that was good.)

Then, driving home, my truck's transmission had a problem: I could shift it into only third and fourth gears. No first, second, fifth, or reverse. Fortunately I-10 between Phoenix and San Berdoo is pretty straight and flat, so I was able to limp to my sister's without too much worry. When I got to my sister's, her husband at the time took a look, and apparently all of the bolts that mate the shifter to the tranny had fallen out over time. It only took about a half-hour to fix, and then I was back on my way home to Yuba City.

I did this whole trip with under $100. I had to stop and get gas in Sacramento (about forty miles from home), and I was literally looking under the seat cushions, grabbing pennies to buy two gallons of gas to get home.

Next time I'll tell you about the trip to Atlanta, Georgia. That was fun, too.

But this fear of responsibility. Where does that come from?

Email to Therapist

November 20, 2003

My mind is splitting right now. I can actually feel the effects of my mind separating from itself. My heart is racing and I'm dizzy. I just cut myself because that usually grounds me, but it hasn't worked.

It feels like the back of my head is spinning…a literal tingling sensation going on within my head…but the front of my head…the part of the brain behind the eyeballs is trying to stay in sync.

I feel like a caged animal, with rage wanting to smash the monitor in front of me to a million pieces, but there's an element of humanity stopping me.

I feel like I want to run outside and start howling at the cold night sky, much like a wolf…there's another part of me that wants to curl up underneath my desk where it's dry and warm.

I'm going to go take a trazadone and go to bed. I will call you in the morning.

Overwhelmed by Paper

December 8, 2003

I'm not sure what happened to me. When I was working at the insurance company I'd routinely have piles of files on my desk. And each file would have to get looked at, its stack of papers resorted, more paper added to it, reshuffled, and then re-filed. It was the most tedious part of my job, but one that I was happy to do most days, because it required the least amount of thinking. I could just hum quietly to myself and play with my paperwork without a care in the world. On particularly slow days, I even managed to email or surf the web while doing it, with no unforeseen consequences. But nowadays, my heart and my head start pounding, my hands get all clammy, and my legs get all shaky when I see a pile of paperwork that I'm supposed to sort through.

A few days ago this happened again. I was doing some work for Monique and I about lost it. This isn't even about the day that I had a complete breakdown because of some QuickBooks training, this was about sorting a few credit card and bank statements.

There's no place to work, really, so I have to sit on the floor, not an ideal working environment for me in the first place, but it's all we got. For me, being on the floor is just ugh. Nasty is the only word that comes to mind. My back and legs ache quickly from being in an awkward position, because there is no comfortable position for me to be in while on the floor. It takes less than fifteen minutes for me to lose circulation in my legs and for my feet to become prickly. Probably half the reason I don't do something as simple as sit-ups or push-ups is because I'd have to be on the floor.

So that's the first issue I had that morning. The second issue is my own incompetence – I'm sure I'm sorting wrong. This is one of those dichotomies that Dr. Geiger has been telling me about.

First off, at a certain level I believe that sorting through bank statements (e.g. putting them in chronological order) is beneath me. Why, I have a degree in business administration, I have an IQ of 130, I'm a fucking genius. Why should I be doing something so mundane? But then the other side kicks in — it really must NOT be important if I'm allowed to do it. I'm the guy who screws up everything he touches. This sorting is probably just a way to have me do something so that I feel somewhat useful, but if it had any bearing at all on the work for the client, Monique would do it herself.

So with that kind of set-up, my self-esteem is already kicked to the curb before I even pick up the papers, and my anxiety level has already increased.

Now I begin to second guess myself. Am I sorting these things correctly? I've always felt that if something was too easy for me, I was doing it wrong.

One of my earliest school-boy memories was in preschool or kindergarten. We were given outlines of a boy or a girl (depending on which we were) that we were supposed to color in, and basically create a self-portrait. The instruction from the teacher (Ellie, I think her name was) was for us to print our name on the top of the page. For some reason I thought it was a trick question, and after I printed my name above the boy's head, I asked Ellie, "Is this okay, Ellie? I printed my name above the boy's head." And I remember she just had this look about her like, "Why are you bugging me with such an inane question?" And I felt about three inches tall. Because I second-guessed myself and clarified the instructions, I felt like a total dumbass.

So nowadays sometimes when I feel like I want clarification of something, I decide to hold back asking and tell myself, "Of course you're right. You're a dummy for thinking you were wrong."

So I look at these papers that I'm supposed to sort, and think, "Monique's quite capable of putting it in date order herself, why would she ask me to do it?" So I think, "Maybe there's a particular type of date order she wants them in." Or, "Maybe she didn't say she wanted them by date, but by vendor." And the anxiety increases exponentially.

Fortunately, on this particular day, I was able to remain somewhat calm and the anxiety only released itself in yelling at the dog (who was stomping on the papers) and a few tears. In times past, I'd have thrown the papers up in the air and have screamed about what a lowly being I was. But I'm still a far cry away from when I would sing a happy little tune. And, anymore, I admit, when she asks me to do some sorting, my first gut reaction is anxiousness. It's a very visceral reaction. I think now I can keep myself grounded and do the work without any ill-timed outburst, but that first reaction still concerns me.

December 2, 2003

What kind of freak am I? What kind of person subjects himself to being cut by his own hands? And not only that, but sometimes enjoys it? I'm not sure what kind of freak that is, but that behavior has become commonplace for me.

I first started cutting about two years ago. Sure, I'd held a razor to my wrist once or twice before that, but never did any tangible damage. But on that morning in October I just couldn't deal with life anymore, and I took a knife and ran it over my arms a couple of times.

And it felt good. I felt relief, pains being released. As bizarre as it may sound, it felt wonderful.

And right now, writing about it here, I crave it. I crave seeing the blood slowly drip from the wound. It's really pretty cool how it doesn't start to bleed instantly, but how I have to sit and watch it start to form along the slice, and then slowly start to pool, and then follow gravity's path down the arm, leaving a nice trail of crimson behind it.

Family members, therapists, friends, have all asked me, "Doesn't it hurt?" Often there's no feeling with it at all; I somewhat zone out as I'm performing my little "ritual." Other times it's an exquisitely delicious pain akin to ripping a band-aid off your skin — you know that pull is going to hurt for a few brief seconds, yet you look forward to it. I guess it's also similar to the feeling that's produced when eating hot peppers. Yes, there's a pain to it, but the endorphin rush more than makes up for it.

For me, cutting is often the only way to feel those endorphins. There's nothing in life that motivates me anymore. I can spend eighteen hours of the day sleeping and wish that I could sleep for the other six hours. I haven't experienced what one would call "joy" in years. Cutting is sometimes the only thing I look forward to. And, in my opinion, cutting is very liberating. At one time I looked at myself and thought, "You know, I don't really have too much to fear. If I ever got into a knife fight, I know I could survive." Granted, I don't know I'd survive if someone stabbed me, but there's the bravado of knowing that a couple of slashes on the arm won't stop me.

And that's the irony of it all, in a sense: I'm willing to hurt myself, I'm willing to deprive myself of pleasure, but I have confidence knowing I can survive. Survive what? There's nothing to my life but an empty shell.

There are a few good people who might be lost without me for a little while, but in reality they'd be better off in the long run. There are a few more people who might be like, "Wow. Stew's dead? Bummer." But the great majority would say, "We didn't know he was still alive anyway." That's my life. And yet, I actually go to some lengths to preserve it.

My cutting ritual is actually pretty comical in a sense. I find my knife — a Wilkinson sword that I use for all types of chopping in the kitchen — and I wash it real well with soap and hot water, then I towel dry it. I take my lighter (if I happen to have any booze in the house, I'll first douse the blade in rum or tequila) and I run the blade through the flame a half-dozen times — must get it nice and sterilized, don't want to run the risk of infection now, do we?

And then I typically proceed with thirteen cuts, about eight on the left arm, and five on the right. Why thirteen? I don't know. It is mom's favorite number (she was born on the thirteenth) and it just seems like an appropriate number. Oddly, if I were going to keep with my favorite number, it would be eleven.

Afterward, I wrap my arms up in towels and wait a few minutes. Then I put some ointment on the cuts (again, no pesky infections for me) and bandage up whatever needs to be bandaged up.

And this is the "joy" in my life. What kind of freak am I?

———

That year was so hard, for both of us. I struggled to understand, to help. I accepted the cutting as a necessary action. It helped him, and there were far worse ways he could have chosen to cope. I was glad that he didn't turn to alcohol. He always said that because of his size, he could never drink enough to become drunk. And while he enjoyed the occasional beer, he was more interested in the science of brewing beer than in drinking it. And drugs? The only drugs were the prescribed ones, and he had no desire to try anything else. So cutting? As far as I was concerned, it was the better option.

December 1, 2003
Journal Entry

It's difficult for me to imagine what it must be like, to hear voices where there aren't any, to see things that aren't there, to wake up, like he did this afternoon, not knowing who he was or where he was.

He went to the store, and while there the voices began again, just behind him, saying his name. He fears he's losing his mind, and he wanted to just stay right there and collapse into himself. The voices follow him. He drove back from the store in the dark, and he doesn't deal well with the dark anymore. He can't see well in the dark, the shadows are worse in the dark. He's afraid he'll lose his license, and I tell him not to worry, that he won't have to drive at night anymore, if he needs to go anywhere when it's dark I'll take him, I'll be here, that he won't have to drive at night anymore.

I tell him it'll be okay, though I have no evidence to support that. He doesn't want to lose what mobility he has. He doesn't want to lose his mind. He doesn't want to lose the somewhat tenuous hold on reality he can still claim. I don't want him to lose any of that either.

Sometimes he doesn't remember things that just happened. Sometimes he doesn't remember when he's had a really bad episode. He's always surprised when I tell him about it later. I don't tell him with the intention of letting him know, I don't realize he doesn't remember. But he often forgets, or it has passed out of his mind, or it's one of those things that he can't afford to hold onto, though he's glad when I tell him. The experience itself, perhaps, is something he cannot keep with him.

I can't imagine what it must be like to hear voices when none exist. And still he retains his sense of humor. We were walking Honey earlier this evening, and I was behind him and chattering about something — who knows what — and he said, "I'm hearing those voices again," and I said, "Hey, that's me! You're supposed to be hearing that!" and he laughed.

When I tell him I don't hear voices so I can't imagine what it's like, he tells me that I hear voices also, but I just ignore them like I ignore everyone else. And he laughs.

We make morbid jokes about insanity and schizophrenia and BPD. Anyone listening to us might think we were insensitive and cruel if they did not know that he suffers from schizophrenia and BPD himself. We can joke and talk like that because he does have it, and it helps to keep the horror at bay. Making fun of the big bad monster makes the big bad monster somewhat benign, or at least not as malevolent, not as scary. But it is scary, it is malevolent, it is spiteful and mean and unpredictable.

We take it one day at a time. The meds help, but they don't eliminate it. He has gotten worse; better in some respects — less prone to psychotic episodes — but still, it seems the shadows and the voices are worse, the distractions, the ability to drive at night has definitely become worse. His ability to function is better, as long as he stays within the necessary guidelines, and I think that is from practice, from experience, from learning what is possible and what is not, something that is obtained only from time spent living with the disease.

And we continue. We live our lives. He does the best he can. That is all anyone can ask, isn't it?

Later that month, we watched "A Beautiful Mind." People kept telling Stew that he should watch it, including his spiritual advisor. He'd tried to watch it by himself, twice, and could not get through it. It was too upsetting for him, struck too close to home perhaps, brought up issues that are hard to face.

Like: They don't do coma shock therapy anymore, but it's frightening to know it's a possibility.

I told him we could watch it together, that I would be there just in case. And so he brought the DVD over to my house, and we settled in to watch. He sat in his chair, the chair that was his when we were married, and the chair that is still his, as no one else except Dog uses it. I made myself comfortable on the couch, and in this position, I face away from him.

Occasionally, during the movie, I'd ask how he was doing, and he'd say he was doing fine. I reached back once or twice to take his hand and he seemed calm.

Towards the end of the movie I heard him — a noise, a sound — and I realized he was sobbing, wretched heartbreaking sobs. I went to him and knelt in front of him, and I told him that I was there with him, that it would be okay, and asked if we should stop the movie. He said no, that he wanted to get through it, and so I sat there next to him and held his hand while we continued to watch the movie.

He was better after that, and we made it through the movie. I'm not sure what happened after the movie. It didn't really matter, all that mattered was that we had watched the entire movie and he broke down only once.

———

My Experience with *A Beautiful Mind*
By Stew

When I first heard about the movie, I dismissed it as some quasi-chick "feel good" flick that I had no interest in watching. Biographies in general don't much interest me; biographies of old teachers really don't interest me.

It wasn't until the movie came out on video that I started paying attention to it. Somebody told me that it was about a guy with schizophrenia. Interesting, I thought. I have elements of schizophrenia at times. And then my spiritual advisor, Rad Peterson, really encouraged me to watch it, so I rented it on VHS.

About an hour into it, I really couldn't take it. I was uninterested, and the sound quality of the tape made it excruciating to watch. But I did feel a bit of kinship with John Nash. Again, Rad encouraged me to watch it. I hemmed and hawed, but kept it in the back of my mind, until my parents watched it on DVD.

So I thought I'd try again, and this time rented the DVD version. This time I was able to get through about an hour and a half, and again I was overcome by how much I identified with Nash. I told Monique my troubles with watching it, so she agreed she would watch it with me. So on my third attempt, I watched the movie all the way through in one sitting.

It was about at the point where Nash had been released from the hospital and he's sitting in his living room and he asks his wife, "What do people do?" that I lost it. I started with a massive sobbing attack, because that summed up a dilemma that I felt I had: What do I do with my life? How do I live? What if I live to be seventy, eighty, or ninety? Who is going to be around to help take care of me?

This wasn't the first time I identified with a character in a movie so deeply. One of the Star Trek movies, Nemesis, I think, had a deep effect on me. When Data died, I sobbed for about twenty minutes non-stop. I felt as if a brother, or a best friend, had died. So for me, identifying with John Nash wasn't that unusual, it was just very deep and profound.

I don't see people like Nash did in the movie. At worst I see shadows at night, moving out of the periphery of my vision. Like when you see something out of the corner of your eye, but then you focus on it, and it disappears. I routinely have that kind of sensation at night, and unfortunately it happens a lot when I'm driving. The other sensation I have is that of somebody just speaking my name — it usually comes from behind me and to my right — and usually when I'm in a store. At first I would spin around to see who was calling me, but after it happened enough times, I've learned that it's not real, though it feels very real.

———

Our days were long and hard. I wondered why I never seemed to get any work done, why I was always behind. Our days were a series of incidents. They were consistent only in their inconsistency and the level of panic they engendered ranged from a one to a ten. On a scale of five.

December 11, 2003
Journal Entry

I'm in a grumpy mood today, spinning my wheels, not getting anywhere with my work. I chat with Schizo Boy online, we go over a few things that are irrelevant, then he tells me he doesn't want to be melodramatic.

And I ask, "What's wrong?"

"The devil is standing behind me. He wants me to hurt myself."

Hurting himself is not uncommon; he usually cuts across his forearms. "Tell him no. How does he want you to hurt yourself?"

"Slit my throat."

"Tell him no."

"He's showing me he could do it himself with his claws. He has point-ends to his fingertips, and he keeps showing me that he's drawing it across my throat."

"He's not real, he's not there. You know that, right?"

But he doesn't know it. He knows it on a rational level, the level that the rest of us operate on, the level that he is on sometimes, but right now he isn't there, and he doesn't know that the devil is only in his mind. He knows that the devil is there, and that the devil wants his throat slit. And how can you fight the devil?

He decides to come over. He'll be here in a minute. And I tell him I will keep him safe. For today, I can keep the devil from him.

And it was normal. Each day was navigated depending on how bad the demons were, what the voices were saying, where the mind was at. I may have lost sight of what was normal and what was not during this time. Visions, hallucinations, voices, these were fairly normal and to be dealt with as one would deal with any other problem that could occur during the day, such as a paper cut.

January 2, 2004
Journal Entry

I had such high hopes for this year. 2004, I mean. And here it is, the second day, and I find myself...well. Let's just say that so far, it isn't quite what I'd hoped. I do take comfort in the knowledge that there are 363 days left, however.

Schizo Boy has been put safely to bed, in my bed, since I provide care best in my own environment. A warm bath and extra meds were prescribed by his doctor when I called him.

Let me start at the beginning. There is always a beginning, if not an end.

This year was to begin with hope, new beginnings, and a new start. (We have a new start every year; sometimes every day, but that is not the point.) However, the day before the new year began, my car broke down. This is not unusual for me. My last car is still hanging around, the transmission shot, totally useless. So I bought another, almost two months ago.

The engine is dead. Possibly the transmission too.

Sigh.

What is one to do? The dealer does not care, of course. It is my problem, not his. I understand his point. After all, I bought it "as is" though I had assumed that "as is" meant it would be running until it was paid for, which would be a year. (I am often sadly mistaken in these things.)

Schizo Boy is not taking this well. Neither am I, but that is not a primary concern. He wants to do damage. First he wanted to kill the car dealer, who kindly offered to give me a break on making the payments on time. He said the car dealer deserved to die. I disagreed, and told him I would not be averse to calling 911 and having him removed to the hospital. Stew, not the car dealer, obviously.

He tried to give me his car keys, said it didn't matter if he had a vehicle or not. I refused, rather politely I thought. He did not take that well.

I made him sit down. I have this strange power over him. I think it's the threat of calling for reinforcements that does it. I called his therapist and asked for advice.

"He won't come to the phone, will he?" the therapist asked.

I looked over at Schizo Boy, who was clenched so tightly I was afraid he was going to explode.

"Sweetie? Do you want to talk to Dr. Geiger?" He shook his head no, as I had expected.

Dr. Geiger suggested an extra dose of meds, a warm bath, and sleep. I asked Schizo Boy if he was willing to do this, and he nodded almost imperceptibly.

"Call Dr. Williams if necessary," Dr. Geiger said, "if he needs to be hospitalized. Call me if you need to."

Dr. Williams is the psychiatrist. Dr. Geiger is very helpful, very nice. Schizo Boy reminds Dr. Geiger of himself at times, which I believe Dr. Geiger finds troubling. Wouldn't you? All the same, he has been much more helpful than the last therapist.

I asked Schizo Boy if he still wanted to hurt someone. He said no, but then, with clenched teeth, said he would, however, go to the dealership and destroy every car there. I suggested that would not be a wise course of action. I can be annoyingly calm at times like these, it comes from experience.

I guided Schizo Boy to the bathroom, after running a warm bath for him. I left him there and went to his apartment to get his meds. I wasn't sure exactly what was needed, so I brought along his entire pharmacy. I returned, gave him a tablet which should help him sleep, and asked if he was feeling better.

He said no, he wasn't, and that every car would be destroyed. Maybe not tonight, maybe not tomorrow night, but it would happen.

There are times during a psychotic break when the patient will utter things that he will later have no recollection of.

He said he would not take a nap after his bath. I told him he would. I sat down in my living room and called his parents. No reason, really, and I don't like bothering them with this because they do worry, but there are times when I just need to hear a rational voice, to get that support that can only come from dealing with the rational, and there are times when I just feel so alone.

While I was talking to his mom, he came out and sat down. She asked how he was, I asked him. I have no problem talking about him in front of him. Nothing too serious, of course. She agreed that causing damage was not a helpful thing to do. She said to let them know if there was anything they could do.

I wanted to suggest that buying me another vehicle might be a good start, but decided against it. Transportation today is a non-issue.

Schizo Boy had not eaten yet today, I didn't think, so after getting off the phone I asked if he wanted anything to eat. He said no, and then asked what I had. I listed a few things, none of which were suitable. I suggested some hot tea. Not acceptable. Hot chocolate? That was met with some approval.

While making it, I found a box of those tiny chocolate donuts that are 95% toxic, and asked if he would like some. He said that would be good, so I gave him hot chocolate and tiny chocolate donuts.

After a while he agreed that a nap might be a good idea, and wandered off to bed.

And now he sleeps. And I ponder my next move. Work? Search for a rebuilt engine that I cannot afford? Clients? Break down? I know! I'll write another chapter! And that brings us up to the present. I've decided a breakdown will be a waste of my time, at least. Hopefully, I covered that necessity in 2003.

And so 2004 begins, but I still have hope for the rest of the year. That's why they call me an optimist.

January 3, 2004
Journal Entry

Despite yesterday's evidence to the contrary, Stew is making progress in seeking out other support avenues, ways to keep from being so isolated, options. Last week he started looking for another place to live. He likes his apartment, he likes being close to me (admittedly, it is convenient for me also), but he tends to not see anyone else much, to be closed off and away from people, which only makes his condition worse. And it's expensive, living on his own. Last week he started looking for a roommate, or a house to share.

He found one possibility, a house down in Shoreline that was looking for another housemate. (Well, technically, the house itself wasn't looking, the person who was leasing the house was.) He called her (the leaseholder, not the house), and he explained his situation to her. That he is mentally ill, but he's not looking for a caretaker. That he functions well most of the time, and when he doesn't, he can deal with it or call someone who can, like me.

And she invited him to go down and have a look. I was with him at the time, since we were out doing things and I had no car, but I didn't go in with him. I waited in the vehicle, slept a bit actually. I tend to do that these days, since I never have enough sleep. I can easily nod off anywhere. He was gone for about half an hour.

He talked to the leaseholder a bit, then to Monty, another resident who was painting the rooms that would be occupied by Stew if he were to move in. There are five bedrooms. The one that is unoccupied is in the daylight basement (he prefers basements, lower levels, while I prefer upper), and includes, besides the bedroom, another larger room, a bonus room. There is a separate bathroom down there, and while the laundry facilities there are for the use of everyone else in the house, the bathroom is, ostensibly, his alone. It would be great for him; he'd have room for all his stuff, two rooms, enough privacy to be okay, but still be around people.

He was worried about the stigma of mental illness, of course. All the TV shows that mention people with schizophrenia suggest they are likely to go out and hurt people. Though this is certainly not restricted to mental illness, people see that as a major factor, understandably so. Like anything else, there are degrees of schizophrenia and BPD and depression.

The meeting seemed to go well, though.

They called him later. They'd love for him to be able to move in right away. They liked him, and want him to be the new housemate. They also want someone right away, and he can't do it until the end of January. They had two more people coming to look at it, and if neither of them worked out by not being able to move in immediately, it was Stew's for the taking.

He is, after all, a rather likeable guy.

It is reassuring to see that the mental illness stigma does not extend everywhere.

I once tried to get him to do some volunteer work. He's good with data, with spreadsheets, with analysis, with paperwork. I'd volunteered at a small nonprofit that claimed to be desperate for help. I helped. I did database entry mostly. There was still much to be done, and I became busier personally. I gave them Stew's name and number, told them he had mental illness, but that he was great in a quiet office environment, and quite intelligent. I told them he'd be happy if they gave him a call and asked him to come in. (He would have. I'd already talked to him about it.)

They never called him. They were desperate for someone to do data entry, but not that desperate. I stopped helping them out myself, since they apparently weren't that desperate after all. They wouldn't even talk to him.

It's hard enough for those with mental illness to function in society without the rejection from those who see mental illness as the most important personality trait in someone who can be productive, is willing, smart, and who wants to contribute.

That sentence was way too long.

Anyway, progress is being made. A move may be happening soon. Change is scary enough, but for him even more so. Stepping out from his comfort zone will help, will show him that he is capable of more. It's an ongoing process. It is proceeding as it should, despite the occasional evidence to the contrary.

January 11, 2004
Journal Entry

Yesterday was Stew's birthday. He turned thirty-three. I don't even remember turning thirty-three, it was so long ago. I'm sure I did — I had to in order to get where I am today, of course. I feel so much older than I am these days. Conveniently, it was a Saturday.

First on our agenda was Stew's weekly meeting with his therapist. The therapist had invited me to come for a session before, and this time I went. When Stew had told him last week that I'd come this week the therapist had said, "Great! This will be interesting and fun!"

Interesting and fun? He must have heard that I'm the life of the party.

This therapist has been much more helpful than the previous one. He recognizes aspects of himself in Stew, and he enjoys his intelligence and wit. We'd spoken before, when Stew had dissociative episodes — psychotic breaks — and I've consulted him for courses of action, but we'd never met.

The session went well. Due to client/therapist/caretaker privilege, that's all I'm going to say. This is an area that only Stew can talk about.

After that, we attempted to run an errand for me, but met with little success. Sometimes that's what happens, life's mundane activities that MUST be done. We got something to eat. And then we returned to our homes. His morning meds take a heavy toll on him and he needed a rest. We decided we'd go out later to go shopping, to make the trek to look for cool stuff.

And so later we ventured out into the world again. I had gift cards from Christmas and he had one from his birthday. Two for Best Buy, two for Barnes & Noble. Two of our favorite places. It was a win-win situation all around.

The crowds, well. Let's just say there seem to be way too many people with nothing else to do than go shopping. Rather like us. The other day we'd tried to go to Barnes & Noble, but it was at the end of the day, when Stew's defenses are not as strong, and the gridlock at the Best Buy/Barnes & Noble shopping area, which also includes several other major stores, was daunting. And I knew, like I sometimes know these things, that he couldn't handle it, that the overstimulation would be too much for him, and so we decided to come back another time.

This time the gridlock was much the same, perhaps a trifle less congested, and I believed him to be in a better place. We went to Best Buy first. He ended up getting a computer game, while I bought myself a cheap tax program and a couple of CDs. One mission successfully completed.

Then Barnes & Noble. I had two gift cards for B&N, so I was going to buy him what he wanted and something for myself. After all, I had plenty of gift card money to spend. We went our separate ways because we don't look in the same categories, the same genres. I can often find him in the religion section (Christian fiction), or the literature/fiction section, or new releases. I head for the bargain books first.

Waugh. PD James, Schwarz (*Drowning Ruth.*) Then I headed to lit/fiction, where I found Stew. There I picked up two Virginia Woolf books. Stew ended up with two books. I saw a few more I wanted, but five was probably enough. Stew found two he wanted. He just doesn't shop in the same quantity I do, but he was happy. There was a balance left on one gift card, and I gave it to him to use at his leisure.

He bore the crowds and stimulation well, though needed a break. I needed one myself. We went to our respective homes, and I told him to take a nap. I attempted, once again, to do some client work. I'm always attempting that.

Stew talked to his dad for quite some time. And eventually showed up again. We decided to go to The Keg for dinner, a spendy steak house that we like. (To those of you who are vegetarians, I sincerely apologize for my steak lust. I have tried to overcome it and dabble in it infrequently, but all the same...)

We went early, to avoid the massive crowds that show up on Saturday nights. 5:00 pm. We're like senior citizens now. We don't really care; being trendy is not one of our goals. Having dinner at all is. Not much to be said about dinner, except that the food was awesome, and Stew really enjoyed it. No dessert. Who had room?

And then we returned to my apartment, doggie bag in hand for Dog. Stew arranged a plate for Dog. I had to laugh when I saw that he'd taken a salad plate, put some baked potato in the middle, and then arranged slices of my former steak around it. I half expected to see a parsley garnish. We are not trendy, except to amuse Dog.

We sat around. We watched some TV. I took a nap. And at 10:00 he went back to his apartment, after saying it was one of the better birthdays he'd had in years. He also received email greetings from friends of mine he doesn't know, and he so much appreciated that. He says I know really nice people, which is true. People who aren't so nice find me boring. (None of these friends were local, they were all long distance, and were people I knew online mostly.)

Sunday morning was not so good for me, though I consider it a slight contretemps in my otherwise contented (-seeking) existence. Stew's mother contacted me by IM as soon as I logged into my computer. She often does this. I turn on my laptop and take the dog for a walk while it gets itself going. When I return I find that she's already initiated a conversation, as if she's been waiting for me. She asked how I was.

I said I was fine, knowing that I wasn't the main concern.

She asked if I'd made carrot cake for Stew. The previous week she'd told me I had to make carrot cake, his favorite. Then she'd told me that there was a cake mix in the package she'd sent him. I'd said, "Good, that'll make my job easier," and she replied that no way could I use a package on his birthday. I had to make it from scratch.

So I told her no, that I hadn't made any carrot cake. I'd considered it, but it was far down on the list of priorities.

She asked if I was making one today. Considering what else I need to do, some of which consists of seeing a client and working for others, it's not likely.

She never asked what we'd done for his birthday. She didn't ask if he'd had a good birthday. All that mattered was that he didn't get carrot cake. I felt chastised, as if no matter what I did, it wouldn't be enough. I might as well tell you that Stew has parent issues, and even though they're great and very helpful with support, they still tend to treat him — and by extension, me — as a child. I have parent issues also, with my parents, though that's a different story altogether. I think I have issues with people in general.

Sigh. Stew is, despite his propensity to avoid reality, very wise. He says he does not need carrot cake. He enjoyed the time we spent together, he enjoyed our activities, he had a great birthday despite the lack of carrot cake, which he said all along was not a big deal, if a deal at all.

January 12, 2004
Journal Entry

I'm chatting with him as I write this. On MSN messenger. I have to say that because sometimes people think chatting means chatting. Instead, it is words on a screen, without inflection other than the smiley faces or the frown faces, or the other emoticons that we use in an attempt to make ourselves more clearly understood.

It is only words.

He's having what he says is an intense "psychic" attack, which doesn't mean he's psychic, it means his psyche is being pummeled by unknown forces. He doesn't know what to do — he wants to cut, but he doesn't want to cut — where does he go from here? What next? He's agitated, restless. Driving back to his apartment a bit earlier he saw someone, a big guy, and when he looked again he wasn't there.

We laughed about something the other day, hearing or not hearing something, and I said, "Sweetie, you're schizophrenic, you wouldn't know anyway!" It is good he can laugh, because when he's bad it helps him to remember that it isn't real.

I tell him I can take him to the ER if necessary, and he accepts that as a viable option, but would prefer not to, and wants to try to get through it.

Hospitals are uncomfortable and he has no health insurance. But if it is needed, I do not hesitate, no matter what he says. He's fairly rational though, so I do not press the issue. I can tell that he is rational enough to make that decision for himself.

It's later, and he didn't cut.

He didn't smash things, though he had the urge to. He made himself something to eat, and he ate, and eventually he returned to his balance. By himself. With the help of a clonazepam, but that hadn't seemed to help much at first.

It's not always that seemingly easy. I say seemingly because I'm sure it's much worse than it seems. When he's psychotic he's also scared, and I can't imagine what that is like.

We chat some more, and he mentioned dinner, and I mentioned mine, which I'd had while he was here. He is unbelieving. "That wasn't tonight," he says, and I say, "Yes, that was this evening, just a bit before you left here."

He does not remember that as being today, it's as if he's now a whole day ahead, as if Monday night and most of Tuesday has been wiped off the calendar altogether. He wrote, "I hate being psychotic!"

It's not funny but it was funny, I can't help it, sometimes these things just come out of nowhere, a serious remark that hits me as unbearably funny, probably because of the relief I feel that he's okay, and when I tell him this he agrees that it does have potential for being quite amusing.

He goes to bed, and he's doing well. He has gotten through this incident alone, with only me through chat, and he has done it well.

"I hate being psychotic."

I often involved Stew in my work. It was a way to integrate him into life outside himself, and it meant we had more time for talk therapy (which wasn't really talk therapy at all since I'm not a therapist, and couldn't even play one on television.) Sometimes I'd get a referral for something that was up his alley, like someone who needed to sell on eBay but didn't know how to get started. That was his particular area of expertise. I'd go along with him, since meeting new people was not his forte. He'd do a consult, and we'd get paid for it, and he'd feel a little bit better about himself.

Once a friend asked me to help out a friend of his, an artist who had brain damage and was desperately behind on her bills; she needed someone to help forestall the creditors and tell her what to do next. I met with her at her house in Seattle, and she said she was preparing to move to an artist's colony. I believe she was also having trouble paying the rent. Her art was fabulous; it dealt with seeing patterns in nature. I wrote some letters for her, and since she was worried about moving, I said I'd bring Stew over to see if he could help. At the time, he was still in good physical shape, and might be able to help with that. He didn't like to do it, but he didn't like to do a lot of things. Still, it was an opportunity, and he was always up for an opportunity, even if he was scared to death of leaving his apartment.

When we went to her house she took us downstairs to the basement, which was a standard basement with a low ceiling and an air of mustiness. There were desks in the corners, and boxes of precious belongings.

We looked around, and discussed the move, and then I realized that Stew was being really quiet. Far too quiet. We went back upstairs, and he was in a big hurry to leave. I told the client I'd come back in a few days and we'd go over a few more things.

We walked outside and Stew turned to me and said, "Don't ever make me go back in there."

"What's wrong?"

"I don't know, but there's something wrong in there."

"Where? In the house?"

"In the basement, mostly. But the whole house too. There's something in the basement that's bad."

He looked shaken, as if he'd seen a ghost, though for someone who's used to seeing demons....

"Okay, you don't have to go back there," I said, because he really looked scared, as if there was something lying in wait at the bottom of those basement stairs that only he could see.

Sometimes we'd be somewhere surrounded by other people, and he'd suddenly get a bad feeling — the hair on the back of his neck would stand up and a chill would pass through him — and he'd have to get away from the place, or the people, and when he did, he'd feel better.

I often wondered if he could feel things that were there, but that I, as a "normal" person, just couldn't feel. Maybe he was able to feel things psychically that others couldn't. Is it possible that his mind wasn't off-balance, but that he was experiencing things that were present but unseen to most of us?

The feeling of being close to something bad, perhaps even evil — though I dislike using that term with its boatload of connotations — occasionally came over me as well, and it was a feeling I experienced only when I was around people I didn't know, or a room of people, though the feeling itself may have been from just one person.

Did Stew's mind show him things other people didn't know were there? Were his demons real? Did he receive psychic telegraphs? I'm usually a very concrete person: Show me something and I'll believe in it. I do believe there are things we don't know about that can't be easily explained away, but my experience with such things is limited, and I'm more likely to shrug off the suggestion than to believe in it. Perhaps Stew's meds tamped down the psychic messages so he couldn't hear them, and maybe they were real.

Or maybe he was traditionally mentally ill and it was all in his head. I don't know. I do know that whatever the source, it was hell for him to live with.

———

The Aborted Move
By Stew

January 25, 2004

So a couple of months ago I had this splendid idea of moving. Why would I want to move? I have a nice apartment in a decent complex. I have easy access to my best friend and caregiver, Monique, and I can have my puppy visit whenever I want. My rent isn't too high, and with the complex recently switching to a decent cable company, I have access to the Food Network and Fox News. But still, moving seemed like a good idea.

And I was moving for the right reasons, too. I'd be moving to gain some independence from Monique and by moving in with a couple of other people, I'd be less isolated and I'd save money on my rent. And when I talked it over with Dr. Geiger, my parents, and Monique, they all seemed to approve of the idea.

So it was settled. I joined www.roommates.com and the first place I saw looked interesting. I'd be sharing a three-bedroom house with a woman in her late thirties who was going back to school to study nursing, and who happened to be a lesbian. Now, I didn't entertain any of those typical male fantasies concerning lesbians, I just thought it would be a good choice since I seemed to get along better with women, and the sexual tension of living with a straight woman would not be there. And with her being a nursing student, and my tendencies to cut myself, it seemed like a good match. So I inquired within, but she never responded. So I kept looking.

Another place that popped up in my search was a five-bedroom house in Shoreline that had two rooms available downstairs. I sent the owner an email, and explained to her about my situation and my condition. Wendi responded and said I sounded like a nice guy, but she'd be worried about what to do with me if I engaged in my self-harming behavior. I emailed her back and told her that I didn't need her to take care of me, and to treat me like anybody else. I told her that if she was down with the flu or something, I wouldn't feel obliged to take care of her, but I might go out of my way to get her stuff from the store if I happened to be going to the store (like orange juice or chicken soup or tissues, or whatever.) And that if she was really bad off, I'd offer to drive her to her doctor…and in the end, that's all I'd be looking for too.

I didn't hear from her for a week or so after that. I figured she'd decided she didn't want to live with a person with a mental illness. Which is fine. But then I did hear from her, and she wanted me to call. She invited me to look the place over and I did, and met her and one of the other roommates. The rooms were ideal: A small bedroom, and a large room that I could turn into an office and a living room. Both roommates seemed nice, and I told them that I could move in the first of February. They were looking for somebody to move in immediately, and they had a few other people to talk to.

I got a call a few days later from Wendi and she said how much she Monty enjoyed meeting me and really liked me. I then decided that I could move in on the fifteenth of January, rather than the first of February. She said she had a few more people to talk to, and would let me know.

A few days later, Wendi called and said that they decided whoever could get them money first could have it, but that they really liked me so they were giving me first crack. I told them I could have a deposit and a prorated amount to them the first thing in the morning. They said great.

It was shortly after I gave them the money that I started having some buyer's remorse. When I talked to Wendi and Monty, they seemed more interested in having money than in the actual person renting the room. Monty seemed standoffish, and when I inquired about a rental or lease agreement Wendi said that they've operated without one just fine for a number of years.

It was also about this time that I started noticing that some things that Wendi posted in her online ad were not entirely true. The ad stated that the house had air conditioning. There was no air conditioning in the downstairs area. The ad stated that pets were "not applicable" yet Wendi did have a small dog that yapped incessantly when people came to the door.

There were a few other minor discrepancies between the ad and what I saw as reality but I figured I'd already made the commitment, and I should have checked these things out sooner.

A few days later, I brought Monique down to look at my new place, and though she was excited about the actual rooms, I'd later find out that she wasn't particularly impressed with my roommates or with the neighborhood.

I asked an acquaintance if he could come help me move sometime in the next week. He agreed, and we set up Tuesday to be moving day. On the Sunday before, I called Wendi and asked her if there was any room in the kitchen for my kitchen stuff. She explained that there wasn't but I was welcome to use her stuff.

This disappointed me more than I let on. I like my kitchen stuff. I've got some cool gadgets that I don't use a whole lot, but I know that they're there. And I like my knives. My set of Wilkinson swords stay sharp even after repeated uses on my own skin. They are very much a part of me. But then I thought, well, if they're boxed up and I can't get to 'em, then I can't use them on me. Maybe it's for the best.

Monday night rolled around and I was feeling completely anxious. Even a clonazepam didn't help. I was over at Monique's watching TV while she was out at a client's and I started scratching my leg, near where a scar was...

Soon I was no longer watching TV but in a trance where all I was concentrating was scratching my leg, lengthening the existing scar. I didn't fully realize how long I'd been doing that until the blood started trickling down my leg and I thought, damn, I'm going to have to make sure I don't drip any blood on the carpeting. So I took a paper towel and blotted the scratch to sop up the blood.

Tuesday was moving day. At eight a.m. I went to pick up the U-Haul I'd reserved. The store was short-handed, so what should have taken fifteen minutes took closer to an hour. I drove the U-Haul to the bank to get some cash to pay Jeff and to buy some pizzas, and I went to the store to get some granola bars and orange juice, in case my blood sugar crashed during the morning. I pulled up to my apartment about 9:15, lowered the ramp and got the dolly out. My plan was to get all the boxes into the truck before Jeff arrived, so that he and I could spend time getting the furniture in, and he wouldn't have to help too much. I've helped move people probably close to fifty times in my life and I know the less work I have to do as a helper, the more I remain friends with the people who asked me to help.

So I loaded four boxes of books on a dolly, and started maneuvering it up the few steps... no problem. Then down the few steps, and the boxes tipped over, spewing books all over the grass in front of my apartment.

I called myself a bozo head for not securing the boxes. I reloaded the boxes on the dolly and took it gently down the curb, and again, the boxes tipped over, spewing books all over the parking lot.

I cussed, cursed, and kicked one of the empty boxes down the driveway. Crying, I picked up my cell phone and called Monique. It was as I was talking to her that I realized, again, that I didn't want to move. I felt that nobody had asked me what I wanted, that I was doing this because it was "good for me." And then I started feeling like a loser. That I can't even get a simple load of books into the back of a U-Haul. I started feeling like Mom, Dad, Monique, Dr. Geiger, and Jake would look at me with more disappointment.

But Monique asked me, "Do you want to move?" And when I told her "no" it was a relief. I could change my mind without being ostracized.

Now I have several boxes of books and other miscellaneous stuff to put away. But it's okay. It's home. For now.

CHAPTER 5

Stew didn't want to move. He wanted to do what he thought everyone thought he should do because everyone said it would be good for him.

What do we know, anyway?

His own mind had betrayed him so many times he didn't trust it anymore, and if we all said something was good for him, he'd go after it with the full belief that we were right. As for us, we thought he wanted to move, so we encouraged it.

I was a bit overwhelmed at the thought of trying to look after him when he didn't live close by, but thought perhaps it was time to give him a chance to be more self-sufficient and independent. I didn't want to be an overprotective big sister who wouldn't let him do what he wanted, who would smother him by asking twenty times a day, "How are you?" (But I did. I asked that all the time because it changed so much, so frequently. I needed constant updates on his status.)

Of course he wouldn't be ostracized! That was a lesson he had to learn over and over again. I called Wendi to tell her he would not be moving in. She was quite upset of course, and refused to return his deposit, but I said it didn't matter, we didn't expect it back. His not moving was just as much a relief for me as it was for him. Having him within walking distance makes my life so much easier.

And he loved the dog, Honey. After moving to our apartment we'd lost Jesse, the last of my Samoyeds, and we were dogless for a short period of time. Then Stew had started looking online for a dog, though I said, "No, I can't, it's too hard." But he was persistent. One day he came upon a half-chow half-golden retriever and he sent the link to me. She was lying on a chair, and she looked cute enough, so I told him I'd go out to rescue place and check her out. He was still working, so I went on my lunch one day from work.

When I pulled up to the "ranch," a pack of dogs showed up to greet me. They were all rescues, and they were given free rein to run loose on the property. They were happy, and they clustered around me when I got inside the fence. But one dog stayed back and didn't come close until the other dogs ran off toward the house, which they were also free to run in and out of. Then she came close, the dog I'd come to see, and she was beautiful, sure, but she was also very careful.

This was not a trusting dog. I went into the house and met with the executive director, and the dog, then going by the name of Goldie, came close enough to me to watch what was going on.

I knew this was my dog, and I paid double the cost to help support the shelter. The director said she'd bring her to our apartment Friday evening — they insisted on checking out the environment of any dog they let go. It was no use rescuing a dog if it wasn't going to a better situation, was it?

Goldie was two by this time, and she'd recently had a litter of puppies after being rescued. She'd been found on the mean streets of Tacoma, bulging with pregnancy, and it looked as if she'd been on her own for quite a while. By the time I found her the puppies had all been adopted out.

I renamed her Honey.

Before the director brought her to our apartment, I made the place spotless. I was so afraid they'd find the environment unsatisfactory! I was totally in love with this dog already.

She played a game where she'd snap at us, just a playful snap, like saying, "Hi!" but it could be seen as threatening. She was not an easy dog, and she didn't trust men, and it worried Stew. She was not as close to him, at first, as she was to me, but she was part chow, and they tend to be one-person dogs. I told him that, but he wanted to take her back.

Take her back? Give up my dog? There was no way. I told him to wait a while, to give it a chance, and though he was afraid she was going to bite him, he gave it more time. Before long, he was as attached to her as I was, and when we moved to separate apartments we shared custody of her. Sometimes she'd stay over at his place, and sleep on his bed, and he'd take her for walks. It was good for him, to have someone to take care of, and have a reason to go outside. That, and she's just damn cute too.

January 28, 2004
Journal Entry

We're watching "Law and Order." Another schizophrenic — by which I mean they're often on television as "crazy people" who cause damage, mayhem, and death — who is guilty of something or other.

And Stew says, "I'm not schizophrenic enough!"

It's true. He doesn't fit the standard perception of schizophrenia.

We laugh about it.

"I don't think the CIA is after me. I see shadows at night and hear voices in the grocery store! What good is that?"

The schizophrenic on TV says Bill Gates made him do it. We say, "Well, duh. That's pretty obvious."

What good is it being nuts if you can't laugh about it?

———

Bears
By Stew

February 2, 2004

As a kid, my first and favorite toys were stuffed animals. Especially a stuffed Snoopy that I believe my grandparents gave to me when I was two or three. I carried that thing everywhere. In fact, I think Snoopy — sans nose and an ear — may even be stored in a trash bag someplace at my parent's house.

Even into my pre-teen years I had fun with stuffed animals. When my grandmother took my parents and me on a cruise to Alaska, I brought a couple of toys and purchased a few more on the cruise. The room stewards started playing with them, hiding them in various places in our cabin. It became quite the game during those twelve days. But on the first day, I almost panicked when I couldn't find the eagle I'd recently purchased. It became obvious the room stewards had a sense of humor when we found the eagle looking out of the laundry bag hanging on the door of the bathroom.

So, it really came as no surprise to anybody who knew me when Monique and I started collecting teddy bears. The first one came from my mom's *Christmas around the World* catalog. He was looking just as cute as can be, and mom had ordered one so that she could "demonstrate" it at her parties. He had quite a phenomenal talent: his belly was made of rice and could be removed and heated up in the microwave and then placed on cold toes or sore shoulders, anything that required a warm up. And then after the bag of rice cooled, it could be put back into the bear and sealed up with Velcro.

When we first got this bear I tossed him on the bed and said, "He needs a name." When I looked over at him, he reminded me of a bear rug, and I said, "We should call him BR Bear. BR for Bear Rug."

Monique hesitated, and then she pronounced the BR together, as in "Brrr." It didn't take too much longer for his name to evolve to Bir Bear. Or, officially: Bir E. Bear. Sometimes referred to as Birry.

So Bir was the first and the only for a little while. Shortly after Monique and I moved to Washington, Monique went to Canada, and found a grizzly bear we named Biffers. A trip to Long's Drugs brought home polar bear Ben E. Bear. And while my parents were in Florida they sent home a small black bear that we eventually named Barty.

Birry, Biffers, Benners, and Barty are the four main bears in the collection. But there are about twenty to thirty teddy bears between Monique's place and mine. Most have names starting with B (Bruce, Bill, Bob, Bucky, Leo) (Leo is a lion, but he thinks he is a bear, kind of an identity issue that he's working on.) And the list goes on.

Each of our four main bears has a unique personality:

Birry, the leader. He has what could best be described as a Napoleon complex. He's smaller than everybody except Barty, but feels that since he was first he is supreme commander of all that he surveys. He enjoys eating human beans. (Not beings, beans.) He's especially fond of nibbling on toes. He's quite the chef, having prepared most sauces to go over his beans. For awhile he craved Norwegians. He was once engaged to one of our Samoyeds, Tasha. When Tasha died from heat stroke, I felt more sorry for Birry's loss than for my own.

Since Birry's belly is made of rice he has an inordinate fear of water. He refuses to go outside when it's raining, or to be near the sink, shower, or bathtub. He enjoys car rides, but gets fearful when traveling by boat. He does love flying, however.

Birry's dream is to have a Hummer with a rocket launcher. That way he could drive over most anything, and blow up whatever gets in his way. I wouldn't say Birry is violent, but he does believe in taking things that he wants by force. And he wants most everything.

Religiously, Birry believes in Big Bear Guy in the Sky. Birry would describe himself as being the second most powerful being in the universe, but he's not sure which powers Big Bear Guy in the Sky has that he doesn't. Birry participated in our wedding as Bear of Honor.

Birry calls Monique and me mom and dad, and my parents are grandma and grandpa. Birry has a unique wardrobe purchased by his grandma, and a wardrobe box built by hand by his grandpa.

Biffy Bear, aka Biffers, is the anti-Birry. Biffers is a sweet, easily excitable, vegetarian grizzly bear. He's substantially bigger than Birry, but much less domineering. He's Birry's right-hand bear, and he takes notes at all the bear meetings, and is usually in charge of decorations for the massive bear conventions that are held at irregular intervals.

But Biffy is not allowed to cook. Several times, Biffy has hurt himself with fire and heat-type implements. Whenever Monique and I are out and we see a fire engine heading in the direction of our complex, we instantly assume that Biffy has wandered too near the kitchen again.

Biffers is not as afraid of water as Birry, and makes an excellent traveling companion. Biffy has been in two countries and three states and has traveled by car, ferry, and plane. But don't let him drive. He becomes too distracted by the pretty scenery and before you know it the car has zoomed out of control and off the freeway.

Biffy refers to his mom and dad as mother and father, to his big brother Birry as Bir Friend, and also has quite the shirt collection from his grandmother.

Benners Bear, aka Polar Bear Ben E. Bear, is the general in charge of Bir Bear's armed forces. Benners greets everybody with a salute and a "yes, ma'am," or "yes, sir." Benners is the most durable of the bears and the largest. He fears nothing, except an attack by Honey Bear the dog. Benners is the only bear to have been chewed on by the illustrious Honey Bear, and has some scars to show it.

Polar bears weren't always welcomed in the tribe of bears. For a while, Benners was looked at suspiciously by Birry and Biffy because of the allegiance that polar bears have with penguins. And we all know about the massive penguin–bear distrust of the late 90s.

Benners believes that my truck is his command vehicle, and like Birry, wishes for a Hummer. Benners has his own pet, a stuffed husky named Tabasco.

Benners' favorite food, other than beans, is pizza. He'll do anything for a pizza. And if we order one, he's likely to scarf it down before anybody else has a chance at it.

Some of the clothes that are a little large for Birry fit Benners just fine. His favorite shirt, though, is a Jamie Moyer jersey from Safeco Field.

Barty Bear, aka Barty, is an enigma. He's part of the four, but he often gets left out because he's much smaller than the other bears. Because of that, he refers to both Monique and me as tall bean.

Barty originally had an English accent and had a taste for tea and crumpets, but over the past couple of years he's been corrupted by the other three and now enjoys the taste of beans, pizza, and bean pizza. Barty wears a small Hawaiian flowery shirt that he stole from Vacation Bear. (Not to worry, Vacation Bear still has his swim trunks.)

So, that's pretty much my family. It's almost unbearable.

————

The bears were able to do all the things Stew couldn't do and through the bears, Stew practiced behaviors and attitudes that he didn't feel safe with himself, such as confidence. The bears were confident and outgoing and scared of nothing. They were often more real to Stew than people. They protected him, they were always there when he needed them, and he was sure they wouldn't desert him and leave him alone. Except for one of their imaginary forays into civilization, of course.

February 15, 2004
Journal Entry

This, unfortunately, is representative of too many days we've had. Both of us with ricocheting emotions, and isolated in our separateness from the world, we had no one to rely on but ourselves.

Stew messaged me early in the day and told me he was stressed. This was in itself not unusual. We were often stressed. Today, it was the car that was in the shop, and, as he said, "I'm out of Pop Tarts." At which point I feigned great agitation at the very idea of being out of Pop Tarts by typing all in caps: NOOOOOOOOOOOOOOOO, ANYTHING BUT THAT!

I told him the car stuff would be okay. My car was immobilized, awaiting a new engine, and his was making a funny noise, or giving some cause for concern. He called a local garage, and then told me he was taking it down there, and that he was sure it'd be fixed by the afternoon so I could go see a client.

Later he returned with the truck fixed, but upset about the funds needed to pay for it. This was a constant. When you see mental illness on television or the movies, they don't show the financial implications, but they're there, piled right on top of the psychosis and the isolation and depression, and they don't make any of it easier.

He was down. I did my usual "cheer up, everything's fine, go home and rest, everything will be fine," so he did, then I had a meltdown. We often took turns, and as soon as he started I'd recover, and we'd go on from there.

I was so tired of feeling like a drain, unable to pay for simple things like car repairs and food at the same time, and so tired of having to be a constant example of cheerful good humor to keep him upright. We IM'd back and forth. I told him I was sick of it all and sick of his self-pity. He told me to just forget about him and not worry about it. I told him that was a fine idea, seeing as how his parents were helping to support us both during our stay in purgatory. What would happen when I was on my own?

It was a grand sort of self-pity that I practiced. I'd throw myself to the depths of despair with all the enthusiasm of a teenager going to a party. There was no halfway for me; when I was in it, I was in it all the way.

I was pissed because Stew needed, after his harrowing morning dealing with the truck, to sleep. This was not because of the truck, or even because he was upset about the truck, but because his meds made a mid-morning nap a necessity. He needed to either sleep very late, or take a nap a bit after getting up. And I'd needed some help, feeling overwhelmed as usual.

Stew suggested going off his meds, so he could be at least "somewhat productive," and help me out. We argued back and forth, Stew wanting to know what he was supposed to do, me being totally unresponsive and telling him it didn't matter, he couldn't do it, and that I was tired of trying to take care of everything alone.

He reminded me that he'd told me that he was going into a deep depression, this was not news. He was always either going into or coming out of one, sometimes simultaneously. It was an amazing feat that I didn't envy.

And once again, the discussion turned back to his needs. He was tired of fighting his depression, his illness, society, and his own expectations. My ranting and raving made him worse.

But who else could I rant and rave to? I felt as if there were no one else. His parents? They had enough to worry about; they needed to know their son was being looked after. My parents? They thought I was crazy for dealing with it at all, I think, and my mother, though she tried to be upbeat, made me feel worse for being such a failure. It wasn't her fault. There wasn't anything anyone could say that would make me feel better. I felt as if my mother couldn't hear me, often, as if she could only hear the parts that were comforting to her, such as, "I'm still alive, still functioning, yes, still working," and from that she would obtain all sorts of information that had nothing to do with reality.

I was an island.

He wanted to give up. Again. And again. And again. So I talked. I commiserated. I pulled him out of the pit again and again, only to fall into it myself. Makes sense, though. The pit can be a pretty difficult place to get out of, and with all that pulling, one might find herself being pulled in instead of pulling the other out.

The conversation took a turn for the worse, if that were possible, when he gave up. I'd recount it here, but our chats are personal, private, and often in a shorthand that doesn't make sense after the fact. I told him he was just thinking about himself again, and not taking responsibility for his own emotions. Yada yada yada.

I went into my black-and-white speech, how he sees everything as either all or nothing (a typical borderline trait, I believe), but how nothing in life really is in black and white. There are many shades of gray, and he needs to try to see that it's not the end of the world if things aren't perfect, because, unfortunately, things are never perfect.

Another issue that cropped up this special day was that I'd found out that his mother had been telling people that her son had his own accounting business. It wasn't enough I was looking after him, it wasn't enough that he was doing his best to get better, but suddenly, I didn't exist anymore. Now it was HIS business, and what did that make me? I felt so marginalized when I'd first heard this, set aside like a redundant piece of machinery, yet it was MY business, my work.

When I took issue with this, he told me not to blame him; he certainly hadn't told anyone that. But to me that didn't matter. What mattered was that his parents were free to tell people anything they wanted and there was no one to stick up for me. That's how I felt. Like I've said, the force of self-pity was strong within me. No one cared about me, no one cared what I did, endless self-pity for all eternity. It was pathetic.

We talked about how I wished he could talk to his parents about things, the really painful things. Whenever I'd notify them that he'd had a crisis they wouldn't mention it to him, as if he wouldn't know about it, or as if once mentioned and dealt with, there was nothing more to be done. But each crisis drained me a little bit more, whether he remembered it later or not. We talked about communication, how hard it is with people we love.

We talked about guilt, and how it eats away at us, how no matter what we do it's never enough, and how he wanted to run away from responsibility, and how that just fed into his guilt.

We talked about white and black, and the gray areas in between that he couldn't see. We talked about options, how there are always several, not just one, and we talked about being responsible for ourselves.

We talked about absolution, and the lack thereof. We talked about how hard it is to get through the day, how even the smallest task can seem insurmountable.

We talked about setting goals, about starting with little ones. We talked about how difficult it was for him to go to church when he no longer had any suitable clothes to fit him. (My solution: "We'll get you some." I am nothing if not imaginative.) This led to him feeling guilty about spending money we didn't have on pants he insisted he didn't need, and from there he felt guilty about eating too much food, which caused the need for new pants in the first place. It was like a spiral, each solution bringing another problem with it, the way every credit has a debit. We talked about making him a list of tasks, about setting aside one day a week for laundry. We eventually compromised: I didn't insist the dryer be empty at the end of laundry day, and he agreed to wash his clothes.

We talked about personal hygiene. He didn't like to take showers anymore, and was showering maybe twice a week. I coerced him into agreeing to take just one more per week. Small steps. He hated his shower, so I said he could use mine if he wanted. Mine was bigger and better, though my bathroom was smaller.

We talked about how it was okay to spend money fixing his truck, especially since my car was still in the shop, awaiting its new engine, and without his truck, we'd have no transportation at all. (Rather difficult to be a traveling bookkeeper with no means to travel.) He agreed to go on a weekly budget, and while it wouldn't stick (as most things wouldn't), the intent in itself was a good sign. It indicated motivation, an interest in improving, which is far better than not caring at all.

We talked about how it was okay to not solve all the problems at once, how we could just start with a few. We talked about how it was okay to be peeved that he felt like no one understood him, while realizing that they just didn't have a frame of reference to use, that this was outside anything they knew, but that of course there'd be guilt for being mad at people, we just deal with it.

And we took a break from our amateur psychology (is there anything worse?) so I could go to work. He walked the dog, and drove me to work.

Later that day he IM'd again and said he felt fragile. No surprise there. I reminded him that when he's not in a good place, psychically, he tends to have accidents. He falls over, hurts himself unintentionally (as compared to the times he takes a knife to his own skin on purpose.) It was another of those "aha!" moments for him. I told him to be careful so he could stay safe.

He said, "I feel like a guitar string that's been pulled or wound extremely tight. It feels like all my muscles are very tense, waiting for the next shoe to drop."

I told him there were no more shoes to drop. Unless one had an unlimited number of feet, there are only so many shoes available to drop, and we'd been through pretty much most of them already. I knew the feeling well though, there was always something else right around the corner that could go bad and, based on my experience, would.

By this time, by the time we'd had endless conversations throughout this one day, and I'd gone to see a client and come back home, and by that time we'd used thousands and thousands of words, so many I couldn't imagine what more was left to say. It was almost six p.m. Most of my day was not spent earning money, which was why I was perpetually broke.

There is no compensation for the seemingly endless propping up of another human being, but I had the satisfaction of knowing that he was okay for this day. I have found that utility companies, supermarkets, and landlords all prefer cash over personal satisfaction, which makes it, at times, scant satisfaction.

February 15, 2004
Journal Entry

The thing is: I can't remarry unless I'm divorced. Officially, I mean. Not that there are any offers, don't get me wrong. There isn't anyone on the horizon, nor is anything expected for, oh, at least a few months, probably years and years. Still, being married to Stew while not being married to Stew would greatly interfere with the entire remarriage process, should that become an issue.

Then there are the other considerations. Once the disability runs out, he'll need state aid. (Unless I become wealthy very quickly, in which case I'm more than happy to help support him.)

Filing for divorce is something we just haven't gotten around to. It's become a non-issue. We knew where we were, we agreed; it is just paperwork. The packet has been sitting in my living room for a very long time, waiting for us to fill it out. There's nothing for us to not agree on. We're quite amenable; each ready to take over the other's debts, willing to keep supporting each other if necessary, whatever it takes.

But it is one of those things that eventually must be dealt with, so tonight I picked up the packet while we watched "Sports Night" on DVD, and began attempting to fill out the forms.

Obtaining a divorce is not an easy process. Fill this out, fill that out, agree to this, agree to that. Then do that another ten times. File here, file there. Why can't we go to court, say, "Hey, we're divorcing, he's mentally ill, I can't be a caretaker and a wife at the same time," and have it over with?

A paper inside the packet says that there's a free divorce workshop every other Friday. I ask Stew if he'd like to go, since it's free.

He says sure, he can do that. (I figure I can send him, and then I won't have to miss work.) (Well, he is highly functioning.)

I tell him it's not a big deal, but since it's free… I don't want to do anything wrong.

Then I think about it. "But what's the worst that can happen?" I ask. "We have to stay married?"

And then we can't stop laughing.

February 19, 2004
Journal Entry

A short entry for today, as befits a short day. The days should be getting longer soon. I certainly hope so, since I seem to never have enough hours in the day. Then again, am I using all my hours productively? I don't think so.

I sent Stew home earlier. We'd met for lunch, and then he went to the bank and to pick up a book for me. Afterward he stopped by my apartment, and I could tell he was tired, so I sent him home to rest.

He went home, walked the dog, and then logged on to his computer. He wrote: "My eyes are playing tricks on me. I could swear I saw a U-Haul truck parked by my apartment. But it's not there."

I asked if it could have left.

"No. I was walking puppy dog and we were walking towards my place. I looked up and saw the U-Haul," and I thought, "Odd, it wasn't there when we left the apartment. Then I blinked, and it was gone."

What does one say to this? Not the obvious, "Oh, you're just seeing things."

That goes without saying. Obviously he's SEEING things, and he KNOWS he's seeing things. Knowing that doesn't mean he doesn't SEE them though.

I told him I thought he needed a nap. He agreed, and said, "I guess I'm having a schizo moment." We like to state the obvious here at Schizo Manor.

"Yes, that'll happen now and then," I wrote, because it is the truth.

His next sentence cracked me up, as these things tend to do. "It's quite disconcerting, I'll have you know."

Well, that ought to go without saying, too but part of the fun is being able to say these things. Without laughing at it, where would we be? Where would he be? Some days that's all he's got, situations that might not seem humorous to others, but must be, in some sort of dark twisted way because without that, what do we have?

"It's quite disconcerting, I'll have you know." Yes, schizophrenia can be quite disconcerting now and then.

Disappearing
By Stew

February 23, 2004

I'm sometimes not there.

I'm disappearing. This is in the end is what I'm looking for anyway, but the process isn't exactly enjoyable. Lately I've had a number of fantasies where I become somebody else and live a life of complete solitude, where my life has absolutely no impact on anybody else, and where nobody else has an impact on me. That to me sounds ideal. I'm tired of being influenced by others and having my existence cause trouble for the people around me.

But the process of getting there isn't pleasant.

Kim, at the hospital, said to me that she had to constantly focus on me because I'd "disappear." And that threw me for a loop. How does a 6'3", 350-pound man just disappear in a room the size of a large living room? But I guess I had this ability to be quiet and motionless and disappear out of the view of others.

And it's happened to me in other places and at other times that I didn't want it to. Like last week I was visiting Computer Concepts and Sven and Robin were chatting with each other. I came in, and they both nodded "hi" to me and I quietly waited until they were done talking and Robin asked me if I was there to pick something up. I said, sure, if there was something to be picked up, and she handed me a file. And then I guess I disappeared because she and Sven resumed their conversation like I wasn't there. These are a couple of the only people I currently feel close enough to that I can call friends, but I was instantly outside their periphery. Not so much as a "How are ya doing?" from either of them.

Even the post office thinks I'm not here. I forgot to pick up my mail for a few weeks, and suddenly, when I go to check it, all my mail has been removed and there's a note in there saying "Vacant." Granted, trying to get the post office to leave me alone is one of the things I am trying to do. (I'm sick and tired of the Tuesday afternoon coupons for merchandise nobody could ever possibly want being shoved into every single mail box on the entire west coast. I'm tired of the little blue-and-white slips of paper showing me a picture of some poor kid who has been missing for fifteen years. I'm sick and tired of being reminded every week that there is another person suffering.)

So, that feeds into my wanting to disappear. I already am disappearing. Why not make it complete? It's not like there are many people who would even notice. And really, my disappearing would benefit most of the people who would notice. But there's only one problem: I'd know I'm still here.

No matter what I do, I'll still be saddled with the same problem: Me. And even as I disappear to the people around me, I don't disappear to myself. In fact, I become even more aware of myself. I become more aware of my thoughts, my feelings, my disappointments, my inactions. I become increasingly aware of how I'm not accomplishing anything, how I'm getting older, how bad my arm pits smell.

I want to disappear, but I want to do it on my terms.

Financial Planning
By Stew

It seems like in my life nothing gets me more riled up than money problems. I think it's safe to say that most of my deeper depressions are caused because suddenly it appears that there isn't enough money.

I feel I have — or I am supposed to have — a different relationship with money than most people do. I try not to care about it. It's something that comes along every so often, and something I need to use to get the goods and services that I need, but it's not the be-all end-all of my existence. But it is.

I try not to take things for granted, but there are things that I just expect to exist: Food, shelter, running vehicle, internet service, and medications. Those are my life necessities. Without any of one of those, I'm pretty much doomed. Without any one of those, my life ceases to have any functionality whatsoever. Without any one of those, I become suicidal.

That's not too hard to fathom, is it? Food is essential. Shelter is essential. Medication is essential. Nobody is going to argue with those three. The running vehicle and the internet service might be called into question, but let's face it, those are my two avenues to the outside world. Sure, I could live without them, but my life would consist of holing up in my apartment playing video games (not dissimilar to what my life really is, but at least with a vehicle and an internet connection I can possibly interact with somebody other than myself.)

So when something disrupts my ability to have one of those five essentials, I panic. Today I panicked. Money that was there to get the car repaired suddenly wasn't there. I don't know why. Monique doesn't understand why. It's just how it is.

There's a verse in the Bible — in Matthew or Luke — that says we shouldn't worry. God provides the necessities for little birds, and we are much greater to Him than little birds, so wouldn't he provide for us? And I try to have faith in that — in that whatever we need God will provide for us. Perhaps He won't give us exactly what we want, but He will always give us what we need. But sometimes it's hard to have that much faith when things seem so hopeless. And things don't look like they're going to change.

I don't routinely pay bills anymore. I wait until something gets turned off, and then pay it. I've never liked paying bills. It's not the idea of giving somebody some money for something I use. If it were that easy, most things would get paid on time. No, I hate sitting down, figuring out what I have, figuring out what I need, writing checks, finding envelopes, finding stamps, and then getting the bills into the mail. It's too much of a time-consuming, overwhelming process — even more so when you know that what you do have doesn't equal what you need to have. Is it laziness on my part? Perhaps, but it's more avoidance than anything else.

Why sink myself further into depression when I can be somewhat happier not knowing what I have but knowing I have enough to cover whatever gets turned off first? It's a matter of survival in my mind.

And all of this is ironic because I consider myself to be a financial analyst. I could probably save money by keeping better tabs on where things are and where I stand. But the bouts of deep depression occur when I know too much about my own financial standing. And it's not like it takes a rocket scientist to figure out my standing: I get $1,300 a month for my disability. My rent is $700, my car payment is $200, my meds are about $300, and therapy is $400. That puts me at a $300 deficit, and I haven't even paid for food, internet, insurance, cable, utilities, or making payments on any of the debt I have.

Monique takes care of me. She makes sure that I eat and get my meds. But she, herself, has a hard enough time making ends meet. I can't ask her to support me.

Fortunately my parents are in a position to help me a bit. That's where I'm a bit luckier than most people with mental illness or perhaps luckier than most people in general. But still, it is demoralizing being thirty-three years old and asking mom and dad to help pay the cable bill, or whatever. Why would I want to demoralize myself more by looking at my bank account on a regular basis and seeing a big fat goose egg? I already feel crummy enough, thank you very much. Do I need to be reminded that I'm a loser?

And though for all intents and purposes I should be on the street, sleeping out of my truck, I still have disdain for people who do it. I shout from the message boards in cyberspace: Six percent nationwide inflation is nothing, that's been the national average for the past thirty years. (Actually it's closer to 6.3%, but who's counting?) And most economists recognize a floor of three percent for unemployment. (Anything less than three percent could cause inflation rates to skyrocket.) So there's only three percent of the population that is statistically unemployable. (And in my world, unemployed = homeless, though that's technically not accurate. Still, I believe if you have a job, you can probably find a place to live).

So I should be on the street, or at least in my truck, huddled under a pile of blankets to stay warm, and figuring out which soup kitchens to eat at. That really is where I belong. That's how God will provide for me.

And there's always been something romantic to me about that, not having a home. I could give my desktop computer to Monique (she needs one anyway), make a deal to get a laptop with a wireless internet connection, and spend my days at Starbucks, and then spend my nights in my truck. I could get a gym membership so I have access to showers. And I could be kind of a vagabond.

But I like my warm bed.

I don't know what to do.

Despite it all, we had fun. It helped that we both had the minds of children. (That we kept in jars on our desks, as we'd say). Playing Secret Spy at the grocery store was not uncommon. You would think a person my age would outgrow that sort of thing, but you'd be wrong. Playfulness cannot be overrated for making difficult situations easier. And if I could make him laugh, the loss of my grown-up dignity didn't matter in the least.

February 21, 2004
Journal Entry

We stop at Top Foods because I need oil for my car. I'm breaking in a new engine and I have to be careful with it, check my fluids daily. And Top Foods markets many things in addition to the customary food items. Like automotive oil. And stuffed bears and other critters, for example. I have difficulty finding such an assortment in stores devoted to such things, but Top Foods is well stocked.

There's a bin of giant stuffed animals. These animals would tower over a child, perhaps causing nightmares. I am unsettled myself, seeing them confined to the big bin. We pull them up and set them so they're climbing out of the bin, ready to make their escape. Other customers look at us as we do so, but apparently we don't care.

We find smaller bears, stacked on a shelf, and we ask one where he'd prefer to be. He points to the next aisle, to the Easter baskets, and so we transport him there, and place him in a basket. Or attempt to, he's a bit larger than the basket, but he is happy.

We move on to another shelf of large stuffed animals; they're stacked haphazardly, as if no thought was given to their comfort. They're upside down, in each other's way, butts in the air and limbs askew. I set about arranging them neatly so they're happy, and manage to knock over the display of boxes next to them. That's okay though. Boxes are just boxes, after all.

When I'm done and the critters have given their approval we move on. A Cat in the Hat display is horribly unfair to its namesake, but as I set about trying to set the Cats straight I see why. The Cat in the Hat cannot, under any circumstances, sit or stand in any way recognizable as sitting or standing, so, in the end, they're just shoved back on their shelf horizontally.

Back to the bears who lost one of their own to the Easter baskets. Another one jumps into my arms, seeking freedom from the drudgery of the bear shelf. We wander, surreptitiously, bear clutched tightly to my chest. I'm sure no one will notice that we're headed for the cereal aisle. Why we're headed for the cereal aisle is a mystery, but we end up there all the same.

Bear sees his target and jumps for it. Inexplicably, it is the Captain Crunch section. Boxes of cereal are cleared out of the way, and bear takes his position right in the middle. Boxes are put back in around him, and bear throws both arms over the boxes to either side of him, protecting the Captain Crunch from those who would dare to buy such a thing.

He salutes us as we wander off, knocking one box askew, but it's okay. It lends a certain air of carelessness, as if the entire scene were accidental and not carefully planned.

We meander towards the checkout. We're not certain if we've been spotted yet, but we'd rather not be banned from yet another grocery store. Eventually we'll run out of stores, which is why the revolts are never staged in our own grocery store. That, and our grocery store does not have a large supply of stuffed animals.

Along the way we find a display of smaller bears, and when I look at one I see it has a plastic pack of some sort attached to it. I look closer, and clearly said plastic pack should be INSIDE the bear, and not hanging outside of it. I pick up one of his peers in an attempt to figure out the mystery of the bear, and find that the plastic pack should indeed be inside, and that its purpose is to make the bear snore. As everyone knows, this is totally unnecessary since bears are capable of snoring on their own without any problem.

Attempts to place the plastic pack back inside the bear are unsuccessful, and he is left in the care of his peers, who all show the proper concern by staring at him with their beady little glass eyes.

We make for the exit, oil in hand, secure in the knowledge that yet another bear revolt has been executed, if not successfully, at least with enthusiasm.

And the car is running fine, thank you very much.

———

Memories: The Good, the Bad, the Forgotten
By Stew

I don't remember like I used to.

Actually, how can I be sure of that? Wouldn't I have forgotten if I had a good memory or not? Well, that indeed is the paradox, and as Dr. Geiger would tell you, my life is a series of paradoxes. I think that's one of the things he finds so engaging about me. I guess that's also the underlying cause of some of my cognitive dissonance — the idea that what one believes is different than what one thinks. For example, I think I'm a pretty good guy, but I believe I'm one of the worst men to have walked on earth. Weird, eh?

But I'm having problems with my memory. Yeah, I forget the occasional things like taking a shower, doing my laundry, what I had for lunch. But I forget whole blocks of time, too. There will be times when I'm talking to Monique and she'll ask, "How are you feeling now?" And I'm like, "Fine. Why?" And she'll say, "Well you were pretty out there for a little while." And I've forgotten that we even talked a few hours ago, let alone remember anything I was doing or thinking or feeling.

The incident that really comes to mind of a time that I forgot was a couple of years ago, at the hospital. It was shortly after the whole thing with Amy blew up, and I didn't feel at all in control of anything, so I drove myself to the emergency room. Somehow or another Monique found out I was in the ER and drove down. I was in the examining room with her, me on the table, and I remember being upset. I don't recall anything I said, but I remember that she said, "I should put you in the car and drive you off a cliff."

I remember calling for security. I remember pounding on the door yelling for help. But I don't remember a thing I said. (I'm told it wasn't pretty. I'm told it's some of the most horrendous stuff I've ever said in my life.) And I'm haunted by it. I'm haunted by the words I said that I don't remember saying. Words that ended a marriage. Words that broke up the best relationship I ever had. Words that probably still echo in Monique's ears when she's alone at night trying to sleep. And I don't remember a single syllable of them.

And I worry about it happening again. I worry about being so disassociated that my words will come straight from my brain and out of my mouth, affecting everybody in the vicinity and me not being able to control it, nor remember it. Just having to apologize for it, and not knowing what I'm apologizing for.

What's scary is that somebody could come up to me tomorrow and say, "Remember that time a year ago when you said all those nasty things?" And I'd have to believe that it happened. I can't trust the fact that I don't think it happened, because I have evidence that it happened before. And if something happened before, it could happen again, could it not? So maybe there have been times in the past where I let loose with a Tourette's syndrome of jerky comments that I don't remember. That's a scary thought.

What a shame it is to lose one's mind.

Parents Just Don't Understand
By Stew

First of all, let me go on record that I think my parents did the best job rearing me that they knew how. And compared to other parents that I know, my parents weren't too lenient or too strict, they were just right.

But, perhaps that, in itself, is a problem. Maybe there's too much of a "just right" thing.

I've often said that I grew up in a "Leave it to Beaver" style household, although my mom didn't do the dusting wearing pearls. But my dad went to work every day and my mom stayed home and baked cookies. My friends came over and were treated like part of the family. There were never any signs of outward trouble or strife. Sure, there were incidents with my sister, but I was insulated from that for the most part. And with her being eight years older and getting married at seventeen, from the ages of nine to eighteen I was pretty much an only child.

My dad once told me, when I was fifteen or so, that he had never really known drama, at least in a family setting. "We've been pretty lucky," he said, "that nothing overly dramatic or overly traumatic has ever happened to our family."

That would change.

But think about it. Think about being a kid and not knowing strife, or arguments, or fighting. The worst arguments my parents had weren't even the silent treatment, because that was the day-to-day, but a scowl glanced from one to the other. Think about being reared in that environment and then being put into a world where violence and shouting and antagonism and fury is the norm. What would that do to a kid?

How do you expect a child to fend for himself in the real world when he is coddled and protected every day of his life? How do you expect a child to become a man and to stand up to a crooked auto dealer when he never learned how to stand up to the bully in the school yard?

I was always told to control my emotions, and my dad didn't like to see any outward sign of emotion from me. I believe he meant well, as he didn't want to see my emotions get the better of me. But how much in control could I have been? Once, when I was twelve or thirteen, I was supposed to go over to a friend's place to watch a movie, but it turned out that my friend had to go someplace. I was pretty upset, so I picked up a piece of discarded newspaper and tore it in half. My dad had a fit about it, telling me that I better get in control of myself. I was even more incensed by that comment. Some of my friends would have cussed out somebody, or punched a hole in the wall, or kicked and screamed. I ripped a 25-cent newspaper that nobody was using. And I had to regain control!?!

"Crying never solved anything." I heard that a lot while growing up. Well, it did. For me, crying was very cathartic, because all those bottled up emotions had to go somewhere, and crying was a great release. But crying really upset my parents. Maybe it was too much emotion for them to handle. Maybe they looked at crying as being something broken or wrong, but the truth was, most of the times, crying wasn't an indication that something was wrong, it was that too many things were wrong in the past and it had to come out somehow, somewhere, eventually.

Sometimes I look back at my childhood and wonder "What did my parents teach me?" Because, and maybe it's a defect on my part, I don't really remember being taught anything positive, just things not to do. Don't let my emotions get out of control. Don't hit people. Don't antagonize dogs. Don't let this dishes pile up. Don't bother your sister. I'm looking around now, looking for the set of "Do's" and I'm not seeing any.

My mother is a wonderful person, but it's quite obvious she overprotected me when I was growing up. She was the "You can't" person in the family.

"You can't play high school football."

"You can't take your wagon to the ravine."

"You can't go to the store by yourself."

When I was a kid, my best friend was Paul. Paul was a typical boy: he liked to go skateboarding, played with army men, and climbed trees, etc. He also hurt himself a lot. He broke his collarbone a couple of times, his arm once, and had a number of sprains and bruises.

To this day I haven't broken any bones. And most of my sprains have come from doing stupid things.

Anyway, Paul's house was close to an empty field that contained a lot of hills and fifteen- to twenty-foot ravines. Paul and his other friends would routinely take their bikes, their wagons, or whatever they had that was wheeled, and go whooshing down these ravines, and either have the ride of their life, or would spend the rest of the day counting the scratches and making sure their limbs were intact.

I didn't get to go. It was too dangerous.

So rather than counting the scratches on my arms, I got to count the number of guys who called me "wuss" or other fun names.

And I got to hear things like, "Sticks and stones may break my bones, but names will never hurt me."

Bullshit.

CHAPTER 6

There was a client I visited once a week. Every Wednesday, for several hours, I'd go to their office and do what I did. Like most clients, they were not friends, not confidantes, not interested in the state of my personal life, though, like many working relationships, they evinced interest. It was a business relationship after all. But some days I would go into the office and everyone would be having such normal lives, with worry about issues that seemed to me so petty, but which were important to them. I envied them their ability to be carefree. I envied their easy sociability and their certainty that tomorrow would be much like today, that at the end of the day there would be no surprises, and they could go home and not worry about the fragile state of anyone else's psyche.

They were friendly and acted as if they cared, but make no mistake: this was a business relationship.

Some days, during the period of time I worked with them, I was so tired and found the work so boring that I found myself falling asleep. I'd go to work armed with enough Red Bull and chocolate to see me through the day, or what I would hope would see me through the day, but it was never enough. It was not difficult work, not taxing, and didn't require much in the way of thought, which made it boring and thereby increased the chance of mistakes because my mind drifted.

We've all heard it: There are only boring people, no boring tasks. So perhaps I am boring. Shall I deny it? Why? Anyway, I'd be there one day a week, thinking about paying my own bills, rent and utilities, as I did their books, and I was amazed at even their smallest expenditures, because they seemed like such a huge waste of money. Money that could be used for what I considered important things. Like the meds that were an essential part of our existence.

I felt like the people at that office looked at me as a loser, as some sort of lower-middle-class excuse for a person, and I looked at them and saw how they wasted money (which is purely and merely subjective), and time — they really wasted time! — because I never had enough time. Some days I felt halfway normal, and other days I felt hopeless, beyond hope, beyond salvation. Such stability they had! Could they even imagine going home day after day not knowing what new surprise awaited them?

Eventually they let me go. No warning, no phase-out period. A simple phone call one day, "We're going to do it ourselves." They used the excuse that business was slow so they didn't want to pay out excess money if they didn't have to. That was not an argument I could disagree with, even if I felt so inclined, which I didn't. I'd known my days were numbered, and I knew they weren't entirely happy with my lethargic approach. At the same time, I counted on the income from that one client to pay my rent. Living day-to-day, making the rent was always a last-minute sort of affair. And suddenly that certainty was gone. There was suddenly no hope of me being able to pay rent that month, an issue which I know didn't concern them in the least (and there was no reason why it should), but to me it was a big deal.

I let it go without making an issue of it because it wasn't their problem, but even so, it hurt. And I discovered that whenever a void is created, more opportunities are created. I got more and better clients. I did just fine. There's always more work around the corner.

But make no mistake: Work is not a place friendships flourish. It's all surface pleasantries.

I've seen this happen to other people, in other places. We come to rely upon the people we see on a regular basis, even though we're thrown together by circumstances and perhaps, common work goals, but this can only last as long as both parties have a mutual interest. In the end, we're on our own.

March 17, 2004
Journal Entry

Just another day around here...Dear Diary,

After I finished my last post, Stew said to me, "Did I tell you about the tiles that were talking to me?"

He was referring to the tiles in the bathroom at Chevy's, where we stopped to eat after our handbag-shopping expedition.

The tiles were changing color, as if they were in code, and they were trying to talk to him. He wasn't sure what they were saying since he doesn't, as he says, "speak bathroom tile."

When I laugh at this he says, "Well, I don't!"

I would think not.

I gather they were flashing like an SOS, all the tiles in his view. Different shades of the tile color, a dirtyish pink, but flashing shades.

This may sound odd. But when he came back to the table I was ready to go, with my box of half my dinner. He went to pick up the box, which was gaping open, and as he attempted to close it I said, "I don't understand the box. I can't seem to close it. I don't know what's wrong with it."

It was a different kind of box than I'm used to.

"Just hold the box closed," I whispered, "and head for the doorway as if you have a closed box. I don't want anyone to know that I can't close a box."

We barely made it out the door before we started laughing.

March 22, 2004
Journal Entry

A short entry today. Last night, on my way out to see a movie, he had an episode.

A schizo moment, he called it. He was at the grocery store, and there were too many people, too much going on, people in his way, and he wanted to strike out, to collapse in a pile in the seafood section (only because he was in the seafood section, the location wasn't important) and cry, or withdraw, be alone in a sea of people. Psychotic episode number 372. Not that anyone's keeping track, mind you.

He tried to call me, once he got himself out of the store, but I was on the phone. I was still on the phone when he tried a bit later. But when I did hang up, telling my friend I really had to go, and it was also time to meet my date for the movie, I called him back. But first I called my date. He'd left me a message saying he was certain I would kill him because he was late.

As if something like that would alarm me in the least.

Then I called Stew. And he told me about his episode. And he felt better talking to me, had felt better just hearing my voice on my voicemail, a friendly voice, someone he knows won't hurt him and will listen. Often all he needs is someone to talk to who won't freak out over the small stuff, who won't exaggerate and make a big deal out of it all, but who will be reassuring and compassionate.

We joked about getting him a medic alert bracelet, something that said, "in case of emergency or meltdown, call Monique at 555-5555. Or Dr Geiger at 555–5555." (Numbers changed to protect the innocent and the guilty.) I can always make him laugh. He worried about making me late for the movie. He always worries about inconveniencing me, about taking too much of my time, but there's no need for that, and I told him so.

He was safe inside his apartment (safe being a relative term, but the apartment is relatively free of demons these days) with Honey the Dog, and he'd make himself dinner and he'd be okay. And he is.

His episodes do not last long these days, do not require intervention except in very rare cases, and it is often enough that he have someone to talk to. I wish there were others he could call in times of crisis, not that I mind him calling me at all, but I am not always reachable. I turn off my phone at movies, I meet with clients, I go on dates, and he does not want to disturb me at any of these times, though he might leave me a voicemail, sometimes just so he can hear my voice.

Sometimes that's enough. I wish he had more of course, but we can only do what we can. It's all we can do.

March 23, 2004
Journal Entry

He sits in the chair in the corner, and he tells me he wants to take the spray bottle of Febreze that's sitting next to him and spray it in his mouth.

I tell him not to, remove the Febreze from his reach, and ask if he wants a cookie.

A health food cookie. I just had one. They're quite good.

He says he's suddenly having suicidal ideation.

I ask if he's depressed. Leave it to me to ask the obvious.

He says he's not any more depressed than usual.

I'm supposed to be going out to dinner in a bit.

He doesn't know what's going on with him. He cannot describe it or define it.

He asks what I'm doing. I tell him I'm writing this as we speak. He says to be sure I tell you about his shoes.

We bought him new shoes the other day, New Balance shoes because no one carries Reeboks anymore. He loves Reeboks. His old ones were falling apart.

He wore his new ones today, and then, when he came over just a bit ago, he had on one old shoe and one new shoe. When I asked why he said it was because "I don't want the old pair to get lonely." Apparently we're on a rotating schedule to retire the old pair, slowly and painlessly.

I'm going out for pasta soon. I ask if he'll be okay while I'm gone.

He nods, affirms that he'll be okay, that nothing drastic will happen while I'm out living my life. I ask if there's anything I can do, and he says, "No, I don't think so."

He feels, he says, "stuck." Just in general. I wish he could define it a bit better, verbalize what's going on, so I can offer something up, but as it is, I don't know what to say. He has a list of things to do, but says when he looks at it he feels like he's done it all but he hasn't.

I tell him we'll make a new list, in the morning. This should work. We work off a task list I make in Outlook. Tasks for me, tasks for him. I need to add to my list too, and refine and rework his list. He does better with a list, doesn't get lost so much, and doesn't founder in the daily details of living.

So tomorrow we'll make a new list. He doesn't think he'll cut tonight because, as he says, "I'm just too lazy tonight." All his knives are dirty and he's too lazy to clean them. He won't cut with a dirty knife. Lack of hygiene does have its good points.

I'm going out to dinner. He'll go back to his apartment and hang out with the dog. He hasn't decided what to do for dinner yet. I brought him Mexican food for lunch. (I had lunch with a friend and brought him the half of the food I had ordered.)

He asks if we picked up his lithium yesterday. I tell him that was today, we went to Costco this afternoon, and I ask if he's had any yet. He thinks that was yesterday, and no, he hasn't had any yet. I suggest he do so.

He brings me what he calls my "atlas" off the printer. My dining companion wasn't sure of the name of the restaurant, but it's on Roosevelt in North Seattle, between 65th and 80th Streets. When I looked for the address on Yahoo, I discovered about a dozen Italian restaurants in that area. I printed out the maps. When I get close, I'll call my dining companion and find out which one he's at so I know where I'm going. Stew finds this amusing. He would. Even now, he's amused by my antics.

Another successful intervention, we might call it. The Febreze is safe for another day.

Headache Scales
By Stew

I need to write something, but I'm not sure what to write about. I had an attack of the suicidal ideations today, but that's not very noteworthy. It came upon me forcefully, but not too suddenly — like a large wave you see out in the distance when sitting on the beach.

I wasn't terribly worried about it, but for an instant I had an uncontrollable desire to spray my mouth full of Febreze. I'm pretty sure that's not an acceptable mouth spray. It probably wouldn't have killed me, either. It would've just made me sicker than I already am.

I get like that, I've noticed. It seems like the suicidal attacks come when I'm not feeling particularly well. And it's not like I can't tolerate the pain and agony of being sick — I've been through worse — but it's kinda like, I might as well croak myself when I'm sick.

A few weeks ago, after Monique and I had seen "Starsky & Hutch," I had the worst headache I've had in a long time. There are three headaches I remember having in life as being the worst ever and this one goes in the top three. One was when I was at Faith Christian, in gym class, so it must have been eighth grade or so. We were sitting around the gym, not doing much of anything, and I remember complaining, "I've got a headache so bad that it would kill a pig." Like headaches kill pigs or something. It was a doozy. But I think that one was mainly sinuses.

The next worst headache ever was when I was twenty-something. A friend, Phil, had invited me to go with him to the racquet club. We played some racquetball and did some weightlifting, and then he told me that one of the things he did while he visited Norway was to take a sauna and then jump into a cold swimming pool. I thought, "What the hey."

I'd never been in a sauna before, and those things are hot and steamy. I lost track of how long I was in there, but it was too long. Sweat was drizzling off my palms. Sweat glands I never knew I had were opening up and gushing sweat. But it actually felt pretty good.

And then I jumped into the ice cold pool. And it felt invigorating. But I was starting to get a headache. I cleaned up, and bid Phil adieu. And went home, feeling a little queasy and with a significant headache starting to develop. I got home, talked to Mom and Dad, and then went off to bed with quite a monstrous pain in my eyes.

I got up and kind of stumbled into the kitchen and got about four Tylenol. I stumbled back to bed and laid there in absolute misery. It wasn't long before I was praying for death. I probably would've found a way to end it myself if I could've opened my eyes long enough to find something to end it with, but the slightest bit of light in my eyes made my stomach flip.

And then it happened.

My stomach flipped and then flopped.

I barely made it to the bathroom before I started retching up dinner. I don't remember what it was, but it didn't look very good at this stage. And then I heaved up lunch, and then breakfast.

And I couldn't stop. Contents that should have been digested by my system weeks ago were coming up. It was the absolute worst case of vomiting I had ever experienced. And each convulsion caused my head to splinter even more.

Finally, after about seven or eight full body ralphs, my sanity began to return to me. My stomach felt much better, and even my head pain was starting to be alleviated. I went back to bed and was able to sleep rather peacefully.

Fortunately I haven't had to go through that again. On the headache scale that was a ten. The "Starsky & Hutch" headache was about an eight.

———

April 4, 2004
Journal Entry

I'm frustrated. Tired. Worn out. Some days I don't know how much longer I can do this. I'm broke. I'm making money and I'm still broke. I'm behind on everything, and that includes his bills, his utilities, his needs. His disability isn't enough, and his parents send money, but it still isn't enough, and I feel badly that they've paid for my car and its repairs as it is. I know what needs to be done, but I keep putting out fires, delaying, putting off, telling myself it will be better later, that if I can just get through the next few days, the next few hours, I'll have time to deal with it all.

I yelled at him yesterday. I do that sometimes. He sat here dejected and sad and I'd come home after working all day on a Saturday — there are no days off for me right now — and when I asked what was wrong, he said he didn't know. He never knows. I told him to stop it.

He got upset, told me to just not to worry about him anymore then. As if it can be turned on and off like a faucet. He should know. He can't stop himself from feeling responsible for me, another guilt to add to the pile.

He couldn't go to the radio station yesterday, the one where he was to do volunteer research. He couldn't go last week, broke down from the strain of it all. I'd said I'd take him this week, but then work came up, a major project that I need for the money, and he said he'd be okay, he could manage it himself.

Of course he couldn't. By Friday night, he was making himself sick with the worry of it. And I told him, on Friday night, not to go, because I hated to see how sick he was making himself. That doesn't really alleviate the problem, because then he feels guilt for not going, he feels like a loser.

So he was dealing with that yesterday, and I yelled at him, and then he put on the cloak of martyrdom, poor me, I'll just go away and everyone will be happier. I told him to knock it off, to go in the other room, sit down, and think about where he wanted me to take him for dinner. I took a break, and then I took him to Barnes & Noble, and then to dinner, though I certainly shouldn't be indulging in things like books and food. And he said, while we were driving, that he doesn't know why he's scared of everything. He wants to be productive, needs to be productive, but doesn't know where to start.

He's scared of everything there is to be scared of, and some things that aren't.

He told me how he's the worst copier. How making copies turns into a farce with him. He was serious, of course he was, but I was laughing so hard because even then he's funny, I can't help it. But it's okay. He doesn't mind, not this time.

I'm making okay money. I could live just fine on my own. I could support myself, and start getting out of debt. I'm tired of being broke, and not knowing where the money goes. I spend hours every day with Stew, talking to Stew, looking after Stew, time I could spend making money, but there's really no question — if he needs attention, he gets it.

He's sick a lot. Every day. Stomach. Bowels. Intestines. Cramping. Every day. Every time he eats, no matter what he eats. I want him to get checked, but without any insurance he won't do it. He says they'll just tell him to change his diet.

And they would. He eats badly. Hot dogs, pizza, fried foods. I can't watch him all the time, it's not my job. And he knows, on a cellular level perhaps, but he knows, that he has to change his diet. Eat what won't harm him. Now, even things that shouldn't harm him, do.

Every day he's sick. Every day he's tired. Sometimes he's grumpy, sometimes he's in a pit so deep I don't know how to get him out, though I usually manage to at least pull him part of the way up. Sometimes, at night, if he's out in the dark, he sees and hears things. Sometimes during the day too. I think the paranoia is getting worse. He's popping anti-anxiety pills like they're candy.

We go on. I have to stop putting out fires and deal with fire prevention. I'll start tomorrow, because today it's Sunday and I have to go to work.

It's night now. I've been to work and back, Stew fed me dinner when I was too tired to do anything other than lie on the couch. He's walked the dog, he's made sure I have what I need. This is what he does.

And I am tired, but not disheartened. Renewed faith and hope live within me, regenerating as a matter of course, though I cannot say why or how. And it isn't necessary to know. I've always been concerned with knowing why, it's been an annoyance, because sometimes there is no why, there just is, and sometimes the why is not something we want to know. But I stray from my subject again.

He ate carefully today, or somewhat carefully, and has not been sick. I hope it keeps up. He has been sad, depressed, felt like a loser, and I tell him it isn't so, that we all have different needs, different ways, differences, it doesn't make anyone better or worse. The real losers are those who can't see this.

Tomorrow we do it again. We do more than try, we do, and in doing, we hope to do it better. Sometimes I tell him that the importance lies not in the doing of something but in the act of trying, and I believe this. If he is unable to do some things he has not failed, even if he has not done what he had planned, or hoped. It is keeping the expectation of hope and of doing better that is the success. What is an accomplishment, after all, than overcoming the odds? Each day that he can think positively, despite his down times, and each time he can believe me, and each time he can contemplate overcoming, he has accomplished something. He has achieved.

————

The Demons Return
By Stew

April 6, 2004

I'm not sure what they want with me. It's not like they are coercing me into evil, although they do tell me it'd be okay to off myself. But they sit back there whispering things to themselves, things I can't hear except for a constant "buzzing" or humming sound of whispers in the background.

It'd be easier if I knew what they wanted, if they would just tell me what to do, then I can either obey or disobey, and I'd have a clearer picture of who I am. Am I an evil person? The type who listens and obeys demons, or am I somebody who is righteous and strong and shuts up demons?

The evil and wicked that I have done would be heartbreaking to my Lord. I fall into traps of the flesh more than a good person should. Who would want me? I have not and will not sell my soul to the Devil, but I am unworthy of the grace of the Good One.

Demons haunt me like vultures over the dead. Though I am not physically dead yet, my spirit is dead. It's not the death of an unbeliever, for I believe many things. It's the death of the unwilling, of those who are too cynical to trust.

There are many of us here — all with white beards, wearing tattered sepia-colored robes, marching in circles around a desolate place. It's a place of no emotion. There are no tears, no laughter. No gnashing of teeth; that would be far too dramatic. It's a place of understood loneliness, a place that we told ourselves we would be happiest because people wouldn't have to worry about us, nor us about them. We carry our staffs to fend off the occasional vulture, the occasional rat. Yet, we might as well use them to crack our skulls and enter oblivion, but that would be too much trouble, and, as pragmatic as we are, would only create unnecessary pain.

We've created our own dull aching pain. A pain strong enough to make us whimper, but not enough to make us cry. A pain that we've told ourselves we can endure, for we've learned that enduring pain makes us stronger. Or at least it makes us less of a loser.

Some of us have created our own pains so that we have some to carry. We felt like we needed to be mournful of something so we bathed in our own mystic misery. We actually saw the light of the goodness. We knew that there was something better, but we willingly chose to harm ourselves so that we could toil here in the land of sepia cloaks and white beards, because we somehow thought it would make ourselves more believed.

Everybody is lost in the land of white beards and sepia cloaks. Everybody is destined to wander forever carrying their staff, their burden, their suffering in silence. There is no sound in this land. There are no colors. No black. No white, except for the beards. There is sand and sepia — a bichromatic scheme that is neither pleasing nor assaulting the senses. There are no senses.

The demons are taking me there. To the unhellish-Hell.

———

April 15, 2004
Journal Entry

I loathe tax day. Partly because I'm in the wrong line of work, partly because, well, doesn't everyone? I'm not myself anyway, I don't know who I am, but I'm off lately. I haven't been well for several days, and while my spectacular crash of last week is done, it created a lag in the space–time continuum (that describes it as well as anything else.) I've felt sick, I've had a change of meds, I've been weak and dizzy and exhausted, yet I feel emotionally strong. If befuddled. Definitely befuddled. Overwhelmed at times, definitely overwhelmed.

And it's tax season. Yay! I am, of course, behind on all the tax work. Not that I do taxes myself, but I do the supporting stuff. I am at work early, though not necessarily productive. Extensions, last-minute things, payrolls, and I just don't feel well.

He came over about mid-morning, he and the dog. She stayed with him last night because I wanted to try to get some sleep. I haven't been sleeping well and I thought it would help if she weren't waking me up at odd hours of the night. Not that it seems to have mattered.

I'm scattered today, doing too many things at once, just wanting to get things in the mail so I can move on to the next project. He wants to help, and the help I need is just to be here — the first three hours of the day I worked in solitude, and sometimes I could do with a bit less of that. I love working for myself, but sometimes there is a lot of solitude. Especially since I've trained the clients not to bother me with phone calls.

And I'm not doing the best, but I'm working on it and holding up.

He is not. What happens has nothing to do with me, it's an external stimulator, but I won't go into that here. And he breaks down. I tell him it'll be okay and that if he goes back to his place he'll get worse. I tell him to stay, to sit down, that I'll be done soon and we can get out for a bit. I know what's wrong, but there's no fix for it. He thinks it's silly, but I tell him he can tell me anything because nothing is all that silly. And it isn't. It never is, really. Irrational, maybe, but not silly.

I'm still incredibly stressed.

I finish what I have to do, I make a couple of calls, and I need to get out of the house for a bit. We have a list. We'll go to the post office and Kinko's and to drop off a tax return at a client's, a tax return that did not come to me in the mail from a tax preparer on time so she had to fax it to me this morning.

And I feel like crap, I really do. I wonder if I have the flu. Dengue fever. Malaria. Entropy. Something.

We go. He drives. I know what's wrong, and I can't fix it, I can only tell him that there is nothing wrong with his feelings because there isn't anything wrong with his feelings. I empathize, for all the good that does.

We drop off the mail, we make the copies, we head towards the client's office. He loses it in traffic, becoming angry and impatient, frustrated. And it concerns me, of course it does, and I begin to feel the familiar note of hopelessness rise within me.

So I tell him we'll drop off the tax return at the client's, and then we'll get some clam chowder at the waterfront. When in doubt, call on food.

Lunch does not appear to be going well. He's morose, sad, angry, very angry, though he can't define it or say why. He's ready to explode at any time. And he breaks down at the table. He takes his knife, it's only a butter knife, but he takes his knife and he presses the blade against his arm, and I know he can't hurt himself that way and he won't, but I make him give me the knife anyway, and he does, and then he breaks down. I ask if he's okay, or if he needs to leave, and he says he's okay. He goes to the restroom to beat up on things.

When he comes back he says he's okay. And he takes some of the focaccia from the basket and squeezes it tightly in his hand and then gobbles it down. And he does it again. And I laugh. He puts pepper in his Pepsi. He puts his bread in his Pepsi, and then eats it. When he eats his quesadilla (shrimp, we are at a seafood place after all) the cheese falls down the front of his shirt and he cleans it off by putting his jacket into his mouth. I can't help laughing. The jacket is subjected to this abuse several times. I take the ketchup away from him once, unsure what he's going to do with it, but certain it won't be a good thing. Indeed, he had planned on putting it into his Pepsi to see how that would taste.

"You're back, aren't you?" I ask him, unsure.

"I'm having a psychotic break," he announces, and his behavior would seem to indicate some sort of psychotic episode. But all in all, it's better than he was, it's life of an eccentric sort but it's life.

"Are you laughing at me?" he asks, and of course I am, but I'm laughing because he's THERE, because the anger has been released and because he is THERE, and I don't care if the other patrons are finding anything about us odd or not, it doesn't matter.

He's there, back from the precipice. We eat dark chocolate cake with ice cream for dessert, so dense I can only eat a few bites. And when we leave the restaurant I yell out "Tax Day 2004!" I don't know why. I'm just wanting it to be over, another tax day survived.

I've felt better. I plan on feeling better again soon. I planned on it today. I'll plan on it for tomorrow. Until then, I'll just continue to do what I've been doing. Keeping my distance from the precipice and helping him keep his distance as well.

I'd been diagnosed with a litany of annoying things myself, and was overmedicated for awhile, which certainly did not help. I was pinging off the walls all on my own, and add one maladjusted ex-husband, and life was certainly interesting. There was an explanation for everything: my inability to cope was attributed to my own mental illness, as if it were perfectly normal for a person to have to deal with the level of stress I was dealing with. Perhaps it is. Perhaps what I was experiencing wasn't so very different from what other people go through every day. I'm sure some people do, too many people. But when it overwhelms us and we're unable to function adequately, is it the stress, or is it because we are also ill? I think it's the stress, and new and better medications can't change that. A more stable existence would help, but more medications would only complicate the situation. And they did.

April 30, 2004
A short entry

So much time has passed since we started this journey. At times it seemed it would just go on as it had, a ceaseless circle, but we've been making progress.

We have some separation anxiety issues.

I'm not available as much as he's used to me being available, and he misses me. Changes are underway, as they always are in life, and it's dealing with ongoing change that presents some of his biggest challenges. We carry on. We do the best we can. I'm not GOING anywhere, after all, but with changes sometimes it's hard to see that. I have the same issues, so I understand.

He's meeting with his therapist right now. His therapist decided he wasn't needed as much, and has cut back his visits to every other week.

This is also a huge money savings of course. But he's right. I think Stew is dealing with his issues very well, he's self-aware, he has a lot of sadness, anger, fear, frustration — and it frustrates him even more that he doesn't know where it all comes from or what to do with it all — but I think that considering the circumstances, he's doing well with it.

He's definitely borderline, and his emotions can be overwhelming. Meds help, I suppose. I hope so.

The weather is warm today, and it's beautiful outside, and I told him to enjoy his day, not to worry about work anymore. I had him working for a few days, and I know it was hard, but he did it, and I could tell it was stressing him very much. It's not a feeling I'm unfamiliar with after all, but he got through it. I'm taking some time off today myself.

Feeling guilty about it of course, but not so much that it's not worth it. If I don't take advantage of time to enjoy myself now, then when?

There is no time like the present. It's here now, it's what we have today, and I can't put it off until I think I've earned the right to enjoy it because, knowing me, that'll never come. I'll never think I've earned anything if I listen to myself.

I'm going out to play. If the work's undone, the work's undone.

May 5, 2004
Journal Entry

Ever have one of those days? Not me. Never. But maybe today. Perhaps.

Last night Stew called me and asked if he was going to die. Immediately, not eventually. I reassured him that he wouldn't be dying anytime soon.

Post-traumatic stress hit me last night. My brother is coming to town and while my brother is a perfectly wonderful person, I am well aware that I am the embarrassing sister, the one with the falling-apart life. My family would be ashamed of me if I lived in the same town, but fortunately for them I don't. I'm the one with the unexplainable husbands, the one who's broke. This brother has even lent me money. Do you know how hard it is to ask your baby brother for a loan?

People aren't supposed to have to help me. That's supposed to be MY job.

Stew has a migraine this morning. A severe migraine; they've been getting worse. I'm worried, of course. I told him to take, in addition to his anxiety pills and aspirin or whatever, a trazadone, to help him sleep. He was vomiting, that's how bad it was. When he answered the phone he said he was dying.

I reassured him he's not dying, it only feels like it.

I hope he's managed to at least get comfortable enough that he can rest a bit.

Anyway. I don't think my brother has time to see me until Friday, when he's taking me out to dinner or something. Two days late for Cinco de Mayo, but that's okay. My boyfriend's taking me out tonight. He actually voluntarily rearranged his guy's movie night so he could take me out instead. What a guy. Why we must celebrate Cinco de Mayo is not quite understood, but I think it's a good excuse to celebrate something, and he hasn't seen me for almost twenty-four hours now.

Withdrawal may be setting in.

Anyway. I gotta get to Seattle. With any luck the post-traumatic stress thing will die down and I'll return to normal parameters. I certainly hope so.

I had a boyfriend, an actual boyfriend. I'd done the occasional dating since my separation from Stew, a brief fling with no-strings sex, and mostly considered the entire process to be both embarrassing and unproductive, except for the occasional sex (though men aren't nearly as good at it as they think.) "Bah, humbug!" I said to dating. But I did interact with people online because that was often the only time I had to interact with anyone. Boring stuff, message boards.

Stew was such an integral part of my existence that it confused older men, who always asked me how long I intended to do such a thing. Younger men didn't care, because it wasn't a relationship they were looking for. Until I met a younger man quite by accident, online. And he was so fun and so stable. There was both honesty and playfulness in him that was rare, and he added a new dimension to my life.

We eventually, after much hemming and hawing, went to see a movie, at his insistence. I told him it was just as friends, that was all.

But that stipulation didn't last long, and at first Stew wasn't sure what to make of this new relationship. He thought that perhaps this new guy, if he were nice to me, would be good for a bit, but he suspected he wasn't really "the one." I suspected the same thing, since I was so much older and worn out and still taking care of Stew. No one hangs around for that for very long.

But Andrew stayed.

When Stew met Andrew, which was bound to happen, it was just two guys saying hi to each other. Stew kept his reservations to himself, but the possibility of me running off and leaving him must have worried him. Fear of abandonment was one of his triggers, so I made sure to tell him that I'd still be there for him, no matter what happened. And so he accepted it. By this time he was interested in me being happy, and if Andrew made me happy, he was all for it.

Stew was invaluable to the relationship with Andrew. When I had doubts, which were frequent because I was so done with messy entanglements wherein I would get hurt, Stew would urge me to give Andrew a break, to not be so hard on him, to stop looking for reasons to break up.

This is not what people expect to hear, but it is how it was. Even as ill as Stew was, he was still a great friend to me. He was able to move on and wish for my happiness. He'd miss me because I had less time for him, but he made room in his life to accept Andrew. And Andrew did the same.

May 12, 2004
Journal Entry

Stew went back on his anti-depressants yesterday, so the two of us celebrated by having dinner out. Much cause for celebration: After several days without Effexor, the poor guy was transparently psychotic, though he still had anti-psychotics. He'd reduced the dosage of those, in an attempt to make them last longer. And the Effexor had run out altogether. And the other pills weren't picking up the slack.

Whew. Interesting few days there. These things always happen before a weekend, when it's even more difficult to get 'scrips. His psychiatrist did call them in to Costco Friday, but Costco lost them. When he still didn't have any on Monday and couldn't reach anyone he called me, and I called his psychiatrist and had her paged. She had fired him recently, told him he needs ongoing care, so he feels rejected once again. He also tried calling his primary care doctor (ARNP actually), on Monday, but she's apparently retired, so there's no one there. This did not help the rejection theme. The health care facility his psychiatrist is referring him to for ongoing care is unsure they can help him since he is not yet on Social Security and has only private disability right now. And no money. That's the problem. No money.

I was working a charity auction Saturday night, something I had not been looking forward to because of organizational conflicts and the board being unprepared for said auction, and any failures would come back to haunt me, as the person in charge of collecting the money, but anyway, Stew called. He'd been to the store, and was certain people were after him.

Paranoid schizophrenia.

I told him they weren't. I made jokes. I asked him what he had to eat at his place. He looked in the cupboard and started laughing at the mac and cheese boxes because there were, he said, so many. Laughing is good, and I'd rather be around a psychotic who laughs than one who's contemplating homicide, but when he's like that the laughing is scary, too. It doesn't stop, it has an intensity of hysteria in it that hints at deeper, darker motivations. I hung in there and we eventually got it stopped.

And I reassured him he was safe inside his apartment, that no one would get him there, and that I would stop by on my way home with some dessert for him.

When I stopped by later that night, around 11 pm, he was okay, though visibly shaken and unsteady. Okay is a relative term around here. He had on his hooded robe, the one that makes him look like one of those little hooded guys in Star Wars who run around frantically, except bigger.

It's a good look for him some days. I gave him my half of a chocolate cream pie and quarter of lemon meringue I'd been given. He doesn't like lemon meringue, but that's okay. I made sure he was settled, and doing okay, and would be fine for the rest of the night. "No one is after you," I told him.

Which then made him feel unwanted.

Sigh.

We do what we can.

And then I returned to my home, tired, late, just wanting to rest. And Andrew-the-boyfriend was waiting for me, to hold me and laugh with me.

Stew came over to my place on Sunday. I told him to come over and we'd go to the store. He showed up in his hooded robe, a giant Wookie at my door. He thought it was a good idea at the time. I told him it was okay to leave the robe, that we'd go out with him wearing shorts and t-shirt.

Anyway. He crashed several times over the weekend. And I shored him up, a temporary retaining wall strong enough to keep him from collapsing altogether. And Tuesday, finally, he got his meds. Now he can get back on track, continue with trying to put together a life centered around him and not his disability, which should be just a glitch and not the sun his life revolves around.

Day-by-day: That's how it's done, right?

CHAPTER 7

Mental illness alone isn't enough to deal with, when dealing with it. The collateral damage extends throughout our normal lives, tentacles of additional discomfort weaving here and there, no region left safe.

A simple thing like going to the doctor can turn into a momentous event. First, there was the time factor. When was one to go to the doctor, when one was supposed to be working or caring for Stew? Less time working meant less money, and money was tight enough as it was because I could never spend enough time working. Caring for Stew took hours every day. Then there was the money factor. I was uninsured. This is not uncommon, unfortunately, so this is a story that is far too familiar to too many.

But on my eye, my right eye, there was something. Not knowing what it was, I couldn't call it something. It was clear, in a manner of speaking, and glob-like, and remained firmly attached to the eyeball for several days, a rolling mass of gelatinous material that interfered with my vision, which I found to be a necessary sort of thing for getting through the days.

And so I went to our local family practice clinic. They would eventually cut me off and refuse to see me ever again, but at the time they were still allowing me to make payments when I needed medical care. The physician's assistant (PA) looked at my eye. Said it looked okay, but she wanted me to see an eye specialist to make sure, someone who might actually know what was going on. I groaned. Inwardly, but it was still a groan. How was I to afford a specialist? We were at a particularly low point in our available cash balance. The PA said to go, and so I said okay. (The idea that I'm a hypochondriac gnaws at me, an idea that I've had in the back of my head ever since I was young and told that I made things up when I thought I was sick, and so I hesitate to seek medical advice, knowing that I will soon be discovered as a fake sick person.)

Stew was with me that day, of course, he had driven me to the doctor's office because I couldn't see very well. And so they sent me to an eye specialist, and we drove to Northgate to see the one specially selected by my doctor who had managed to find time for me in his busy schedule.

His office was deserted. We were the only people there, which was a very good thing as it would turn out. The doctor came out to tell me his fee was $100, payable in advance, and then he could look at my eye. I looked at Stew and said, "Let's just go," because I didn't have $100. I could have written a check, but it wouldn't have been a good check, so there seemed no point to that. Stew asked the doctor if he'd accept payments. The doctor said no. One hundred dollars in advance, payable now, if we wanted him to look at my eye. No payments, no something down, $100 all or nothing, and we were free to leave if we didn't like it.

I wanted to leave. Stew was adamant that I would be seen. I wanted to go, Stew wanted to stay, the doctor wanted his $100. Stew said he'd pay for it and took out his checkbook. I was familiar with Stew's checking account, since I managed it, and I knew he didn't have $100 either, and so I told him no, not to write a check, that we could just go and I'd be fine (since I am, after all, a hypochondriac) but Stew was agitated, and he wanted me to be seen so we could know if there was anything wrong with my eye or not. He told me to let him deal with it, and so I gave in. Having Stew upset was not worth it; his angry moods were overwhelming and frightening. He paid the doctor his $100 with a bad check, and the doctor said he would see me now, and I went back to the exam room. He flashed a light in my eye, he spent all of five minutes with me, and then he said it was nothing, it would resolve itself in a few days or so, and if it did not, to return, pay him another $100, and he'd take another look.

I felt scammed. I understand the whole "paying for services rendered" sort of thing, it is not foreign to me, and I understand doctors have expenses, and I fully expect to pay for services received, and I most certainly want to pay my own way and be a responsible adult, but at the same time, I felt scammed.

No matter. The important thing was that the suspicious eye problem could be chalked up to a harmless anomaly and was nothing to worry about. Didn't help with my immediate vision problem, but all the same, it was a relief.

Until we got back home to my apartment and the doctor called me. On the way home we'd come up with a plan to get the funds in the bank to cover the check, perhaps a parental loan, perhaps a payment I'd get for services rendered to a client, I'm not sure, but we had a plan to cover the check. It didn't matter. The doctor was already on to us. He'd called to verify funds, found out they weren't available that day, and he was irate. He yelled at me. He told me he would have my friend arrested for giving him a bad check. He ranted. He raved. I ranted and raved back. It is not one of my finest moments, my ranting and raving, but it comes now and then nonetheless. I told him we'd have the money in a couple of days, but he was not to be soothed, or placated, nor reassured. He wanted his $100, and he wanted it that minute. Did he think I'd print it up myself right then?

Behavior like that might indicate that the good doctor himself was having a cash flow crunch, or maybe he just didn't trust lowlifes like us who expected free treatment. I hope it was the latter. Doctors should not be that desperate for a hundred bucks.

We once pawned some of my jewelry in a fit of desperation when we needed enough cash to buy some food to get us through the weekend. I felt as I did with the doctor: incompetent to run my own life, irresponsible, a blight on the face of society, too humiliated to face life straight on, or to look anyone in the eye and pretend that I was like them. The fact that many people face the same sort of problems every day did not help, because at the time, for all I knew, we were out in the world alone. This is not the sort of thing one shares with others, and it is not the sort of thing people bond over, at least not people like us who are trying to give the impression we are like everyone else. And sometimes, though I now have health insurance and a better income, I still feel like an imposter.

It's tough out in the world without money. When we'd pawned my jewelry it was because all of our bank accounts, except my business account, had been slammed closed by our bank. They were fed up with our continued overdrafts, though I always got them cleared up. But they'd had enough, and we were out somewhere and found, quite unexpectedly, that suddenly our cards were worthless. Both of my checking accounts, and both of Stew's, were closed, and only my business account was allowed to continue its existence. I had to resort to writing a check that would later bounce, but we'd already eaten and how else were we going to get out of the restaurant? I was so ashamed. Since we had no money for a few days, we went to the pawn shop. I'd never been to one before. I pawned the rings from my first marriage, which weren't worth much, and later some other jewelry. None of it was all that valuable, but it got us through a few sticky phases.

I also sold my Wedgwood china, my crystal, and my silver during those years. I sold everything that someone would pay for. None of it mattered as much as paying for living expenses.

Relationships with money are so varied. Money can define who we are, where we rank in society, how we're regarded by others, and how we think of ourselves. I thought of myself as a loser because I had no money and was in debt. I'd been financially responsible since I'd left home at eighteen, never asked anyone for anything, but splitting up with my first husband was the start of years of financial instability and poorness. Not poverty. Even as bad as I felt about it, it was never absolute poverty because I always had services I could sell. I'm good at what I do, and that saved my butt. So not poverty, with no hope of getting out of it. But desperation. A lot of desperation and a lot of debt. And a lot of shame.

My doctor's office cut me off. When I got sick I had to go to a walk-in clinic and pay cash. My therapist — the same therapist Stew had — cut me off. I wasn't as worried about that as I was about Stew. People looked at me funny and would point and stare. Little kids would avoid me. Or perhaps I just imagined those last two.

This all sounds rather desperate and sad, and at times we felt desperate and sad. But there was more than that. I don't believe in the saying that God never gives us more than we can handle because sometimes, if He is giving out things, He does give out more than people can handle, and those people crack under the pressure. They throw themselves off buildings, or they jump off a bridge, or they shut down, or they hurt others, or they just stop. People get more than they can handle all the time, depending on your definition of "handle." What does that mean anyway?

We worked with what we had and sometimes, we had fun. Sometimes we laughed about being mentally ill, and about how the world we lived in was so different from the world everyone else lived in. Though everyone's world is different from everyone else's world, isn't it?

146

I never threw myself off a building with the desperation of it all, but there were times when I considered it a viable option. However, it wouldn't have helped Stew in the slightest. He'd still be out there alone, and it wasn't as if I had life insurance that would pay off. Besides, I never wanted to die. I just wanted to have enough money to get him some help, and to be able to pay our living expenses without panicking when the end of month rolled around.

The heartwarming stories about how someone conquers mental illness don't tell you about what happens when the mentally ill can't get support to help them through the rough times, when they end up homeless and alone, and when their caretakers, overwhelmed by their needs, end up in bad shape too. Caretakers aren't much mentioned at all, are they? But we're out here anyway.

But every time he had a good day, or a good hour, or he could see a future without pain, it was all worth it. We were family, the two of us alone out there, and when it's your family, you do what you can.

May 31, 2004
Journal Entry

Someone called me a heroine last week. A heroine.

I don't want to be a heroine. It disturbed me. I was disturbed the rest of the day, and well into the night. I don't want to be that. I'm not that. I'm just me. I'm not a heroine.

What is a heroine? And why do people think that? Somehow, doing what I want to do has turned into this. And I just want a semi-normal life. Normal altogether is out of the question. That wouldn't fit my psyche, would it? But semi-normal would.

It's been my experience that heroines come in, save the day, return things to some sort of order, and then everyone goes on to live happily ever after.

Except the heroine. What's she supposed to do now? What happens then?

The heroine must go on and do good again while others are settling into comfortable domesticity or finding peace.

This particular non-heroine just wants to live her own life.

Well, I do. Obviously. But being a heroine leaves no room for just living. I've gotten better at thinking of myself, though I still feel guilty about it. There's only so much I can do, after all. Thinking about myself first has never been a priority because it was never something I deserved. Which is just plain stupid. Of course I do. It's a difficult thing to change though, when one is accustomed to not deserving.

I don't want to be this heroine people imagine I am. I'm not. I'm just doing what needs to be done at this time, I like to think it's what anyone would do, though I know, realistically, it's not. I know this because I've been told this by people, by therapists, by those who see it happen elsewhere. People don't do this, but the fact that I do does not make me a heroine. It's just what I do.

I don't want to be known as someone who saves people. Sure, I like saving people, when they need to be saved, it's part of my history because I'm not sure I'm worthy if I'm not helping others, but that's not my purpose here. What is my purpose here?

I don't know. I suppose, like many people, I just want to make a difference. But what does that mean?

I'm not a heroine. I'm just me. And I can be pretty selfish. And self-centered. And totally un-heroine like. To be heroine-like now and then is easy: It's thinking of what other people need. To give them that does not interfere at all with what I'm doing.

Okay, sometimes it does, but so what? It all comes down to choices, doesn't it?

I choose to not be a heroine. I choose to just be me. If I do something worthwhile in that phase, that's good. But I am not a heroine. I'm just me, and the me that I know is not at all heroine-like.

Let's try this again.

Instead, I am self-centered, and interested mostly in my own preservation, like most people. We have to be, because if we don't save ourselves first, we can't save anyone else later. I did what I could for Stew because I just didn't consider not doing so to be a choice. How do you walk away from someone who needs help?

I do it all the time now. I see people on the street who need help, and I walk on by. But I don't know them, and I can't save the world. I would if I could, but I can't. I could barely save myself and help Stew to save himself. I didn't save him. He saved himself.

May 26, 2004
Journal Entry

Practicalities. Our mental health services suck. Stew's psychiatrist fired him because she wanted him to get more regular oversight of his meds than he could afford to go to her for. He has a therapist, and all he needed from her were 'scrips. But no, she wanted him to get ongoing care with her, so she fired him.

Try telling someone who's depressed and has borderline personality disorder and recurring demons accompanying the paranoid schizophrenia that people aren't avoiding you when even your psychiatrist sends a Dear John letter.

Anyway, she recommended Compass. They offer services on a sliding scale. Hah! We went there yesterday. He was terrified, so I went along. We met with their office manager. He would, if eligible to be seen there for med management, be responsible for 50% of the cost, which can be $150 to $200 for a visit. He has no insurance of course. No help from DSHS (The state of Washington's Department of Social and Health services.) His private disability will be running out before long. A large chunk of this goes for meds and therapy/psych. The rest is supposed to cover rent, food, living expenses. Well, it doesn't. Anyway, DSHS says he makes way too much money to qualify for med coupons.

They even sat there and told him he's one of the people who "fall through the cracks." Why? He has too much money coming in. Not enough to live on, of course. When will be he eligible for more services? When he's homeless and the private disability checks stop. Then he can get help. Until then, they say get some private insurance. How the hell is that supposed to happen?

Uh huh. Sucks. I figure it's up to us to make sure he can keep an income coming in, but getting there is a bit of a pain in the ass. Working on it, though. I know it's possible for him to make enough money to support himself; we just have to get the right thing going and keep him at it. Some days I feel like opening my own vocational rehab. That's me. Vocational rehab, onsite support, ongoing personalized therapy.

Stew did eventually get food stamps. That helped.

Overloaded. Yes. So I'll deal. But sometimes, just sometimes, I get this feeling that if I'm not doing everything for everyone, that if I have my own problems, that if I need something from someone, that no one will love me anymore. And that sucks. And I'm told it's not even true, that I don't have to do more than everyone else to be thought half as good. I don't know why that's stuck in my head as solidly as it is, though.

Yeah, I'm getting better at giving it up to someone higher up — learning to trust that what is supposed to happen will happen, and that it's in someone's control who is better at this stuff than I am. Slow process for me, but I'm working on it.

An email sent on August 5, 2004 to Stew's parents and Jake:

The following instructions/helpful tips are issued to concerned parties in preparation for the Stew-and-Jake upcoming moving expedition, in which Stew will drive down to California with Jake in order to move Jake's mom to California, and then Stew will come back to Washington with aid from his dad. Personally, I would love to have a road trip like this to look forward to, but I am trapped in this apartment with a pile of work.

Later we'll talk about Stew's dissociative episode the other night.

But first, we have prepared the following tips on the care and feeding of Stew.

As you may know, Stew has anxiety (severe at times), depression (major), and a mild form of schizophrenia. And borderline personality disorder, though he does have one of the less toxic forms of this. And I think he's bipolar. No, maybe not. Anyway. Let's just say that Stew has a few issues, okay? We'll just leave it at that for now.

If Stew seems a bit out of it, it's quite all right to ask him if he's taken his meds. His meds are important for his functioning, and he's pretty good about taking them, but occasionally he forgets, or runs out, though we do try to avoid that.

Stew hates the heat. Hates it. Makes him grumpy. You don't want to deal with a grumpy schizophrenic, believe me. If it's particularly hot, he may seem spacey. Remind him to drink plenty of water and/or Gatorade. And to eat properly. He says that's not usually a problem, but let's try to avoid too much bad food.

Migraines. I think that these are exacerbated by heat. If he starts to get a head ache, his best bet is to go to a cool dark area for a few minutes and take his migraine meds. Hopefully the migraine will subside in thirty minutes to an hour, but there is the possibility that he'll have to rest for up to eight hours.

At times, usually at night, Stew may or may not see things that are or are not there. This is a byproduct of the schizophrenia. What Stew really needs is reassurance that there is or isn't anything there — depending — and that it's safe to continue. He needs to know he's not, for example, running over anything or anyone. His hallucinations often manifest in the late evening, when he sees shadows or movement that isn't there. Fortunately, he's usually cognizant enough to know that the thing really isn't there, but it still spooks him. (Imagine: You see something or someone, and even though logically you know the thing or person isn't there, can't possibly be there, there is still the fact that you see him/her/it anyway. Rational thought is difficult under these circumstances, yet Stew does it pretty well nonetheless.)

Stew snores. Have him wear his Breathe Right® Nasal Strips if it is bothering you.

Stew has demons. Really. Life-size, real, honest-to-Bir-Bear demons. Sometimes they, or it, stand behind him, or keep right behind him if he's moving, where Stew can't see them. They sometimes whisper things to him that are harmful, philosophically or morally. And sometimes they suggest things that are harmful physically. I've found the best way to deal with these demons is to make fun of them. They're not nearly as dangerous as they make themselves out to be, nor as scary, but they must be dealt with firmly and purposefully, resolutely and with scorn. Remind Stew that the demons, while frightening, have no power over him, no matter what they say. When speaking to the demons themselves, use a calm voice and/or ridicule. Do not buy into their logic.

Stew self-harms. This means he may or may not hurt himself intentionally, usually by using a knife. This happens infrequently and is not likely unless he's alone. (In other words, he won't start brandishing a knife in your presence.) Do not be alarmed. As a dangerous activity, self-harm is highly overrated. Stew knows to sterilize his knives well and clean up after himself. There are far worse behaviors he could be exhibiting, so please keep this in mind if it should happen. And don't panic. Really, there's no need to even become upset. If he disassociates, sometimes cutting helps him reconnect again. Sometimes it helps to refocus the pain and sometimes it serves as a distraction. Just talk to him calmly and assure him that everything is okay.

One more thing. There is 24-hour telephone counseling available by calling 555–555–5555. Technically, while this is advertised as 24-hour, there may be times when the counselor is not available. If she's with a client, say, or in a movie, or asleep and doesn't hear the phone ring. Still, feel free to call this number at any time so the counselor can either guide you through what to do with Stew next or talk to Stew personally to talk him down from whatever heights of panic he has reached. Or up from whatever depths of despair he has fallen to. In the event the counselor is not available, Stew's therapist may be called, but he's not nearly as good at this.

Stew does not want to disappoint anyone: it's one of his biggest fears. He's stressed about this impending trip not because of what it represents, but because it's a change from his normal routine and change is scary. Between worrying about disappointing anyone and the stress of change, he might be a bit on edge. I've found the most effective approach is to soothe and reassure. Should he be truly impossible, threatening to kick his ass may result in long-term improvement but with the possibility of short-term repercussions that will make things worse before they get better.

Call me anytime.

August 10, 2004
Journal Entry

It's been days since I've posted, as you no doubt have noticed. Time is fluid around here, it ebbs and flows unpredictably.

That, and I tend to get rather lazy now and then. Let's call it laziness and be honest about it.

Stew is preparing for his road trip, and he's rather nervous about it. Since Jake is legally blind, he can't do any of the driving. So that part, on the first leg of the trip, is all up to Stew.

He's told me he won't make it, that he won't last. And he has been sick a lot. Retching, mostly, nauseated a lot, headaches, and it's been hot, which doesn't help matters in the least. I told him he'll be fine.

I know he doesn't want to let anyone down, and he worries about that. There are so many things that can go wrong, after all, but that's the case with everything in life. Unfortunately, that's what he sees so often. I want him to go and have a good time. Spend time with Jake, see his parents, have fun.

The other day he said that when he gets back he'll really get to work on his business.

Overall, he's been holding up pretty well. Had a bad time one night last week, disassociated, cut himself, called me late at night. We talked on the phone and I did my best reassuring come-back-to-earth spiel, or at least what I could at the time. It exhausted me, so I can't imagine how it exhausted him. If it does that to me, what must it do to him? And then he gets frustrated because he's so tired and doesn't feel like he can get anything done.

The next morning I was still worried about him. Even though he said he was better after we'd talked, it's hard to tell at times. I called him, and there was no answer. Both phones. So, assuming something needed looking into immediately, I ran (drove, actually) over there. Only to discover he'd been in the shower and was doing much much better. That's quite normal. There I am, still in the trough from the night before, while he's moved on to other, better emotions. It was such a relief that he was okay that I didn't pummel him too badly for not letting me know sooner. Besides, he's bigger than me, and pummeling must be performed with caution.

Today he helps Jake and Chris pack up the U-Haul. I hope the heat isn't unbearable for him. Other than the physical demands, it should be an okay day. Even that is an unknown though, since he is so often physically ill these days. Tomorrow they head off to California. And Dog can come stay with me for the duration. I've missed Dog, as annoying as she is.

That was a hot day, that day they packed up, so I worried about how Stew would handle it. Halfway through the morning he called me and asked me to come get him. He was sick, and he had a headache, so I drove up and got him, and he went home and rested. And the next day he was able to go on the trip.

I always encouraged these sorts of things. I told him it'd be okay, that he'd be okay, and to at least try. It was so very difficult for him to go through with anything that varied from his daily routine; sometimes his daily routine was more than he could bear. There was a fine line between encouraging him to try something while letting him know that if he didn't, he wouldn't be letting anyone down.

I'm not sure that's even the right sort of thing to do. My methods were from instinct and experience with Stew. I wanted him to try things and get out because it helped him be better. It was too easy for him to hole up in his apartment and never see anyone but me, and the longer he did that, the harder it would be for him to make progress. He made progress most every day though, even if it didn't seem like it to anyone else.

While Stew was away on his trip to California I frequently heard from his mother. She asked where he was, how he was, how the weather was in the area they were passing through. I felt like the Stew Young Hotline, always available to answer questions about Stew, and she always had questions about Stew.

Of course she did. He was her son, and she worried. But I was tired of being the one who was supposed to have all the answers, the one who served no function other than to be caretaker, and while I understood her need to know her son was okay, I also resented that she (no one, in fact) was interested in how I was doing. It wasn't her fault, or Stew's, it's just the way it was. I made myself a loner because I didn't know how to relate to people, and I didn't want people to know I was weak and needy, so I kept it to myself. What people thought was strength was really me trying to live up to my own expectations, which included not asking for help and not wanting anyone to feel sorry for me.

I can be incredibly selfish, and I'd often think, "What about me?" I still do. I'm still the same ego-driven selfish person, wanting to know who's going to look after me.

The following was written after a chat with Stew's mom. This isn't, obviously, the actual conversation, but the one I was having in my head while the real conversation was taking place. There are, of course, significant parallels between them.

Thank you very much for contacting the Stew Young Hotline. Please hold while our operators search for your victim.

I'm sorry, ma'am. I didn't mean to mumble. I said: Hello, this is the Stew Young Locator Hotline. How may we help you find your son today?

What's that? You're his mom? And you want to know where he is?

Ma'am? We just talked two hours ago.

Yes, I know. He's still driving to California.

Fires? No, he didn't mention any fires, but I'm sure they're okay.

No, I don't know his ETA. It's a long drive, ma'am, and I can't really say.

They left yesterday about 2 pm, stopped for the night, and are continuing on their way today, expected to arrive in Sacramento this evening.

No, I don't know what Governor Schwarzenegger did last week, nor do I care.

What's that? You haven't been sleeping at night? Yes, ma'am, I do believe you've mentioned that on the previous five occasions we've talked.

No, I'm not sure where they stopped to eat today. I didn't press for details.

Why not? Oh, well, I was working ma'am. That's right. I'm trying to support myself here. And sometimes I even support your son.

What's that? How's the cleaning of his apartment going? I think it's going all right. I have, as I said, been out working today so I couldn't stay there all day. Do you want to know how I'm going to pay for the work that's being done?

Just as well, since I have no idea how I'm going to pay for it.

It's funny, but I can't get anyone to work for free except me. But he'll return to a place that's livable once again, since the mentally ill sometimes have problems with maintenance. And I'm thinking that will help.

That's right ma'am, I have my own place to look after. Like I've said before ma'am, maintaining two households is not easy.

Yes, I'm quite sure Stew will be all right. No, ma'am, I didn't send anything along with him for you, just him.

Yes, I know you're looking forward to seeing him. How do I know this?

BECAUSE YOU'RE DRIVING ME INSANE!

Oh wait. Sorry about that ma'am. Did I say that out loud? Apparently I'm developing a form of Tourette's.

LEAVE ME ALONE IF YOU'RE NOT GOING TO ASK ABOUT ME!

Sorry? What? Oh, was that out loud also? Like I said, MA'AM! I'M AN ACTUAL PERSON HERE, NOT A MACHINE.

Yes, Stew is with Jake, they're quite all right. Jake is the most responsible person I know.

What? You'll talk to me tomorrow? Ma'am, you've talked to me three times so far today. I don't talk to my own mother that often.

Sometimes, ma'am, I go entire weeks without talking to my mother.

That's right, ma'am. I am a bad daughter.

Yes, ma'am, Stew is just fine. If he weren't, someone would call you. No one has called you. That means that everything is fine.

Yes, no news is good news. That's what I'm saying.

Thank you. Your cooperation is appreciated.

Here at the Stew Young Hotline we exist only to ensure the safety of Stew.

Thank you for calling your Locator Service.

———

Email
By Stew

August 18, 2004

Hi all.

On the trip back, Dad asked me if I had experienced any demons during my stay in California, and I indicated that I hadn't.

I'm currently experiencing demons right now.

They started when I was walking the dog tonight. I had an inclination that somebody was following me, but there was nobody there. In fact there wasn't anybody around, which for 9 pm is a little unusual.

The demon(s) were telling me that I should remove my skin. Not just cut it like I tend to do, but to take a potato peeler and peel away the skin. (I'm not even sure if I own a potato peeler.)

They kept showing me images of how it would feel better (can you really "show" a "feeling"?) if my skin were removed.

The oft-asked question is what was I doing or thinking right before this happened.

I was watching TV. I was flipping back and forth between the Olympics and "Smallville" (not a show I normally watch.) The last Olympic event had been swimming (men's 200m backstroke I think) and the only thing that stands out in my mind about that is that American Olympian recently celebrated his twenty-second or twenty-third birthday. The episode of "Smallville" (it's a TV show about Superman [well, actually Clark Kent] as a teenager going to high school and the misadventures he gets into learning about his powers) is about how one of Clark's friends got mixed up with illegal street drag racing, because it was the only thing he seemed to be good at, and it allowed him to get out of Clark's shadow.

So, that's the status of the demons on August 18, 2004. Whatever that information is worth.

Oh, and no. I did not cut, nor am I inclined to.

I called him when I received the email, about an hour after he wrote it, and he was doing quite well.

CHAPTER 8

This is a hard chapter to write. Not because something horrible happened, because it didn't, but it could have. But I am loath to talk about this kind of thing much, because it's stereotypical, and wrongly so. It is what people expect from the mentally ill, as if they're all deranged potential killers. "Mentally Ill Man Kills...." reads the headline.

Sure, it happens. It's horrifying and makes people think that the mentally ill should all be locked up, put away where they can't hurt anyone. But that's so rare. Most mentally ill people are not dangerous, and if they are dangerous, the person most in danger is themselves. Most of the anger is directed inward, most of the damage they do is to themselves. But yes, sometimes they are dangerous to others. So are non-mentally ill people who kill. And drunk drivers.

An excerpt from an email I sent to Stew's parents on August 28, 2004:

We have achieved stabilization today. Everything's okay, but I thought I'd let you know about yesterday. Stew is rather talked out about it. He'd like to not have to deal with it anymore at the moment. He's been to his therapist, and both the therapist and I have told him that if he seems to be posing a threat to anyone (including himself), we'll have him confined.

I know. It's a very bad thing to think about.

Yesterday Stew took a knife from his kitchen and headed to a political rally, and by the time I found out about it he was back.

As I'm sure you know, Stew has been taking politics very seriously and personalizing it. Though overall he's been getting better, in some regards. However, because he is better in some regards (I can't remember the last time his affect was flat, for instance), other issues arise. (The therapist says this. I'm obviously not an expert but I see how it's working with him.). He's not sure what to do with himself next, and so somehow he becomes, um, a tad bit perhaps maybe homicidal. Oh, I hate using that word.

It's like all the anger that's inside him has to come out somewhere, so that's where he focuses it.

Anyway. There was a problem with the traffic, luckily, so he turned around and headed back. I don't think anyone was in any danger, and neither does his therapist, but predictability is not something we're familiar with. Since my main goal is to keep him safe I have to take it all seriously. He called me on his way back, and it was the first I knew he was even out. Told me where he was and what he was doing, and that he was headed back because there was no parking.

He didn't seem to know why, exactly, other than of course the political thing, but why he's so upset about it, no one knows. He doesn't know, so asking him doesn't bring any answers.

He got home about 8 pm or so, I think, and seemed to be doing okay once I'd talked to him for awhile. In fact, he was easy to talk to and not at all delusional, except that his perceptions are a bit skewed. He wasn't psychotic though, and I can usually tell (not that his actions weren't a big enough clue.) We laughed that he was foiled by a lack of parking (there comes a time when all we can do is laugh or....)

I called him at 11 pm to see how he was. He said he was fine and sounded like it, but said he'd been suicidal half an hour before. We talked for a bit, and he actually sounded good. His moods can change so quickly that it can be a challenge to keep up, but it does mean that his suicidal ideations tend to pass pretty quickly, which is a good thing.

He stopped by this morning on the way to therapy (and delivered one mangy mutt) and was doing okay. After therapy he called me, upset, so he came over and we talked. The session had gone okay, he said, but I think he was upset by what the therapist told him: That if what happened yesterday happens again the therapist will have to do something about it. I told him that I would also. The important thing is to keep him safe, and if he's going to grab a knife and go somewhere with intent — whether or not we think there's any chance he'll do anything — we'll do what is necessary to keep him safe. Then we had lunch and talked about them Mariners. They're not doing so well. (That's not true. We actually talked about me a lot, but that's boring.) He ate well. Had on a nice new shirt, too.

So there we are. He's better in some respects, but there are other things going on, too. It's a balancing act, I think. Or juggling. Or something.

He's supposed to be napping right now. I roasted a couple of chickens yesterday, and told him to come over and get one for his dinner when he wakes up. His productivity is up, he's been feeling better physically it appears, and overall things look good. But we're a bit concerned naturally.

He's been told to avoid the news and I'll keep after him about that. He sees his doctor again Tuesday. I think he has plantar fasciitis. I had that last year and it hurt, but I fixed it by wearing better shoes.

All questions and comments are welcome. He's a bit overwhelmed with it at the moment though, so feel free to ask me. (Not that I have answers, mind you, but you can ask anyway.)

Love,
The Caretaker

————

It was scary to think about confinement, hospitalization, drastic measures, but we do what we have to do. It was a political rally of some sort Stew had headed off to, for a Democrat. Stew was always convinced he was a Republican, and for some reason he got it into his head that this Democratic candidate had to be stopped. So he drove north with a steak knife.

A steak knife, of all things.

Fortunately, he had trouble finding parking when he got there. An assassination attempt by a crazed mentally ill man stopped for lack of a parking space. Stew wasn't the most committed assassin, and he wasn't sure, when asked afterwards, why he felt he had to do this. It was just something he felt he had to do.

I hated thinking about having him confined, but if he were ever a threat to anyone, I'd do what must be done. I never worried about him hurting me, only people who he felt had wronged one of us, or someone that he suspected of wanting to cause us pain or inconvenience. I never really thought, until this incident, that he would take steps.

But even this isn't entirely true. After the episode with the car I had to work with him quite a lot so he wouldn't stomp out and go to the car lot and cause trouble. He was angry, and an angry Stew is a sight to behold.

September 8, 2004

I haven't been saying much lately, have I? It's not that there's nothing to say, it's not as if the entire mental illness situation has gone away, it's not as if I don't want to say anything. I think we've just been so busy living our lives that we've neglected to keep up with bemoaning the sad state of affairs around here. Maybe that's because we're refusing to wallow in the sad state of affairs.

Yesterday morning Stew called me, said he didn't want to worry me. Of course he doesn't want to worry me. He never wants to worry me. But I make him talk to me anyway. He said he was suicidal. He's so tired of being so tired and he doesn't feel like he can do anything. I told him I'd be right over and we could go to the ER. It seemed like that might be necessary, though admittedly there's nothing much they can do there except make sure he's safe, which I can usually handle myself, but there comes a time when I'm not sure what to do, and at those times I resort to the ER. It's been a long time since he's visited the ER.

On my way out, Andrew, the long-suffering boyfriend, told me to take over some pancakes. He'd made us some for breakfast and there were some left. So I took a plate of pancakes and drove over to Stew's. I wasn't overly alarmed. Stew's moods can change so quickly that overreacting too quickly doesn't help anyone. (This had been a difficult lesson to learn, and it had taken some time before I could react with seeming nonchalance.)

As I was looking for a parking spot, Stew called, said not to bother, he was okay. See what I mean? I hadn't even gotten there yet, and already he was telling me not to bother.

"But I'm looking for a parking space right now and I have PANCAKES," I told him, "So I'll be right in." As if I'm going to just turn around and go home after that. Right.

I took the pancakes in and Dog became overwhelmed at the thought of all those delicious pancakes just for HER. Of course. I tell her she can have just a piece of one and the rest are for Stew. She looks at me in disgust, as she usually does when she doesn't get everything she insists she's entitled to. Stew told me he'd talked to his therapist and since he didn't have an actual plan in mind, there was really no point in going to the ER. They'd just talk to him, after all, and his therapist could do that himself. Or me, for that matter. I'm cheaper and I make house calls. I'm not particularly therapeutic, but I can be amusing.

I heated the pancakes, put butter and syrup on them, and gave them to Stew. And we talked. More precisely, I talked first. Not about him and his suicidal ideation, but about me. I'm quite self-centered. My entire life revolves around me, and I want everyone to know about it. It's one of my character flaws.

Then I let him talk for a bit. It's good to share, I think. It doesn't have to always be about me after all.

And you know what? Despite the way he feels and the way his emotions run rampant and the way he sometimes feels so out of control, he's been doing well. He's sick of being sick, both physically and mentally. He's physically sick from being mentally sick, and he's tired from taking the meds, and from the almost constant stomach disturbances he's been experiencing, and he's tired of being sleepy all the time, and he's tired of his eyesight getting worse. Who wouldn't be?

I'd be pretty tired of all of it too. We talked about how, though he feels like he's doing nothing, he really is doing something. He did a lot of spreadsheet work for me in the past week, he has sales on eBay, he takes care of Dog, he is doing things. Sometimes I get so tired I have to sleep, and that's just from me being me, and I always feel like I don't do enough, so I understand how frustrating it can be.

But it's not enough to kill oneself over. I'm sorry, Stew, but it's just NOT ENOUGH. Especially with the progress you've made. It's not enough. And I think he knows that. He'd better. I tell him enough.

We talked. He felt better. And then I left to go see a client. Stew's doing okay, with demons or without. Sometimes I see the demons as impotent little red monsters, trying to make some sort of progress with this guy, trying to make inroads into his psyche where they can cause more damage, but he just fights them off, and he goes on his way, and the demons are mad because they can't get far enough in.

This week he also felt rejected by an agency that deals with people with schizophrenia. As we look for resources, we come across roadblocks. He's not on Medicaid yet, he's still on private disability, no Social Security, and that was one of the requirements for this particular program. I've emailed the agency myself — we're just looking for RESOURCES, for crying out loud, for any information, we're not asking for full treatment or any treatment at all. Two days later, no one has responded to my email.

No doubt they're understaffed, but could someone please just let me know if you can help us find resources or not? I feel rejected by them too.

This evening he went to an eBay group. Drove himself to Seattle safely, though when I talked to him as he was driving down there he was sick again, retching violently, an all too-common problem lately. But he went. And he stuck it out. And when it was over, he left and got himself home. Though it was getting dark and there was a slight problem finding the freeway and he started to lose it, he managed to keep himself together enough to get home. He did well. He learned more things. He did it on his own. He's capable of so much, even with this thing, he's still able to do so much. Perhaps he has to take things slower sometimes, and perhaps he needs to stop expecting so much of himself.

Perhaps we all do. At least everyone else does. I should be expecting more of myself. That's what I think.

At the end of the day, everyone is doing okay.

One day here or there, there's no record of when, Stew was severely depressed and he picked up the phone to call the crisis line.

And then he hung up.

This is apparently a no-no. The crisis line reacts when this happens, and before Stew knew it, there were police at his door. They took him out in handcuffs, put him into one of the police cars that were parked in front of his apartment, and took him off to the ER.

I knew he'd been feeling badly, and so I walked over to check on him, only to find the door locked and no one answering. His truck was still in its parking space, so I knew he couldn't have gone far. He wasn't out walking the dog because she was with me.

I pounded on the door. I tried to look in the windows, but all the shades were drawn. I called Stew's cell phone, but all I got was voicemail. So I sat down on the front steps and I thought about what I was supposed to do next, and I imagined the worst because what else was I going to do?

I was so scared that he was inside and I couldn't help him.

And then my phone rang. He was at the ER and he needed me to pick him up. He never again called the crisis line and hung up on them. We call this a learning process.

October 24, 2004
Journal Entry

I caught him the other day. Caught him in a moment of happiness. Caught him red-handed. We're similar in some ways. Sometimes I forget things and doubt myself, and sometimes, when he's in a dark pit of illness, he forgets that there is more to his life than that. All he remembers, when he's down there, is that life sucks, that it hurts, that there are things that no one can help him with when he needs help, that there are demons out to get him, that he is alone and sad and knows no joy.

That's what he knows when he's bad, and he forgets anything that gives lie to this illusion. Or he buries it or dismisses it as a fluke.

And so I remind him. I remind him when he's in a bad place, and when he's happy and laughing and things are going well I point it out to him, I tell him he's been caught, that life is not all bad and that there is joy in it.

"Damn!" he says, or something similar, or he laughs, and I can tell that he feels almost embarrassed, that he feels as if he's not entitled to be not miserable, that perhaps he's acting inappropriately.

We were only driving to Barnes & Noble to go book shopping — we'd had something to eat, we were going shopping, then back to my place to watch TV. And he was laughing, we were talking and making jokes, and when I pointed out to him that he'd been caught being happy he was almost ashamed, as if his illness should preclude such an event, as if he's supposed to be miserable all the time.

He has just now been declared disabled and unable to work by the State of Washington. He has been unable to work for several years, but that was with private disability, and now that's gone, so now he needs public assistance. And he thinks — I know he thinks, deep down — that as a recipient of aid, he should not be happy, or enjoy life.

This is, of course, absolutely ridiculous, but we are not always logical about these things. While receiving aid makes him feel worse, it can also help him. He is now eligible for other programs, for other aid, perhaps now he'll be able to get help with medical and drug expenses. So far, that's all been out of pocket, at retail, and the pockets are not particularly deep and some of the drugs are particularly expensive. (But they keep the demons at bay and are necessary for survival.)

And perhaps now he can get attention for his other medical issues. His bad eyes. He can't be out much at night by himself, not just because he sees and hears things, but also because he can't see very well. He is sick often, retching and nauseated and in pain. Perhaps his ulcer is back. All of this has been neglected because it is expensive and there has been no health coverage. Maybe, I desperately hope, some of this can be looked at now. I must see a doctor soon myself, but that can wait. It has to. I don't have medical insurance. I need a couple of things looked at and I need a crown. But let's not even go there.

The demons visited him again the other night. They were behind him, hovering. We chatted online about it and I told him they probably just wanted to use his computer, that he should go to bed, get some sleep, and by morning they'd be gone. I think it worked. Of course, the concept of demons being computer literate does not do much for my peace of mind, but it would explain the increased spam I've been receiving. Who else would be involved in such things?

But I caught him being happy, and I pointed it out to him, and we laughed about it, and he was glad to be caught. One of his greatest fears is that he'll be considered not disabled. It's an awkward position. He IS disabled, but he can still be productive and happy and NORMAL, but if he is, it's as if being those things negates being disabled. And if he's not disabled, there is no help for him, he'd be declared "lazy" and "unwilling" instead of unable. I take the position that he can be all those things. Not lazy and unwilling, that's not what I meant. Disabled. Unable to work in a conventional environment with conventional hours. He can still be productive (and IS), he can be happy, though of course his "issues" will mean he'll have more than his share of unhappiness, but he can be as normal as any of the rest of us, wandering around doing our own peculiar thing. Normality is, in my opinion, not only highly variable but also highly overrated.

And it's the little things we have to look for in order to enjoy life. Some days I feel overwhelmed and hopeless and incapable. And then the smallest thing, seemingly insignificant, will make me laugh, or be a positive indicator of things to come, or make me feel safe, and I will feel as if I'm the luckiest person on the planet. I tell him to try to see the little things, because that's what makes up our whole. Happiness does not come in large chunks, but in little pieces, like a jigsaw puzzle, and we have to put it together ourselves.

But I've strayed. I caught him being happy and feeling joy, just doing routine things, and I pointed it out to him. That's my job.

December 8, 2004
Journal Entry

Sometimes it's just the side effects that are unbearable. Anti-psychotics are not particularly good for the system. They may keep the demons at bay, but they also prove quite discomfiting, if not downright unpleasant.

He's sleepy a lot of the time, gets up in the morning to find that he must go back to sleep shortly thereafter. It's constant sleepiness. So it's hard to get anything done, and some people don't understand why he can't do more. His eyes are getting bad, bothering him quite a bit. He's always had floaters, but now he can't see at night, and the shadows that follow him around demanding his attention only make it worse. Since his eyes are bad, he can't even be sure, much of the time, if the shadows are shadows following him around, or if it's his eyes bothering him.

He doesn't know what to do. He must have the anti-psychotics, we know that. He knows that, yet he thought of going off of them for a few days to see if it would help his eyes. That is how it works. That is how schizophrenics go off their meds. Will it be better without my meds? Will I be able to stay awake? Maybe I'll be better now; maybe I can manage without the anti-psychotics. Whatever the side effects are, they wonder, as they must, if there's another way.

Those close to them wonder also.

He feels useless sometimes, incapable of helping out, of earning his own way. I tell him that if it weren't for his help I wouldn't be able to do this business, that my productivity would be greatly decreased, that I wouldn't be able to go out and do as much as it seems I sometimes do. My client load is becoming, perhaps not burdensome since I need the clients, but it can be overwhelming with the conflicting demands. I need the money, so I try to do it all, but being on my own means that with his help I can do more.

He does errands for me, walks the dog when I have to be gone all day or when I can't, like today. I an inner ear problem and I can't get around without falling down. He makes bank runs, he goes to the store, he sorts for me, he does spreadsheets from statements I give him, he writes copy, he advises, he even makes me dinner. He does so much more than he realizes, and I tell him it's okay if he needs to sleep, it's okay if he can't keep up with me, few people can. And he laughs.

He does much more than he realizes. He supports me. He does not let his illness sour him, he keeps up with his meds even when he doesn't want to. He is capable of so much, but it's hard, with his illness and the meds that are supposed to make him better, to see that.

He asked me one day what would happen to him. "What will happen if I live to be old?" he asked me. He's only thirty-two, almost thirty-three, and the prospect of having no one to care for him and help him concerns him. I told him that I'd make sure he'd be okay and cared for, that it was something he didn't need to worry about. Hopefully he'll get better enough that it isn't an issue, but I know there are options for him. There are options for all of us. His schizophrenia is not nearly as bad as it could be, and hopefully it won't get worse. With that, his BPD, and his anxiety and depression (as I say, who wouldn't be depressed with all that going on?), I am impressed at how well he holds it together. I admire his resiliency, and though he becomes discouraged, he is still one of the strongest people I know.

Looking back at this from the safety of 2011, I wonder what I was thinking. I was certain that I had to make him better. I knew that the time I spent helping him was not to be counted as an invalid use of time, nor was it to be mentioned to him as anything other than a good thing for both of us. I needed help doing my job because I spent so much time looking after him. Checking up on him. Spending time with him. Getting him through the difficult times, which were very frequent.

He wasn't the only one who misplaced his sense of reality at this time: I did too. I don't regret that. I couldn't very well tell him how drained I was, how hard it was to keep taking care of him day after day. He felt bad enough, and I couldn't have him feeling any worse about himself. And in order to convince him that he was worthwhile, which he most certainly was, I put myself in the same reality. So we were in the same landscape, dealing with the same issues on a more or less equal footing. Reality is fluid, I think, in that we change our perceptions in order to survive. At the time, I concentrated on him, and I withdrew from the world, because having me out in it while he wasn't just didn't seem right. And in our world, I could justify putting myself last. I became so accustomed to being a caretaker that I thought that was my sole purpose for being. Turns out I was wrong. I was just supposed to be his caretaker, not the entire world's. Andrew helped me with that. He brought me back into the real world.

Sometimes Stew had a flat affect, and when he did, it was worse than having him psychotic, at least for me. For him, perhaps a flat affect was better, for he didn't feel anything then; it was as if he were an empty shell. Talking to him was an exercise in futility. He'd demonstrate no emotion, and he wouldn't respond. If he were psychotic, at least I could tell there was a real person in there. With a flat affect, it was as if he were no more than a robot.

I like robots as well as the next person, but not when they're supposed to be people.

One day he showed up at my apartment in the morning and his eyes were dull and lifeless. I looked for evidence of him inside, but couldn't see any.

When I asked him how he was, he was unresponsive, and when I asked him if he wanted to go get something to eat, he said he didn't care. When I asked him what he did care about he said, "Nothing."

While I blathered on about anything at all, like what a nice day it was or where we should go, he just sat silent and still. I wanted to break through to him, but I didn't know how.

I could have used an instruction manual, but unfortunately his illness didn't come with one.

"So," I said, "what do we do now?"

"I don't care."

"So, what do you care about?"

"Nothing."

That was obvious.

We sat in silence for several minutes, and we would've continued to sit in silence as long as I didn't speak. He wasn't about to say anything without being prompted because he was totally empty, as if the human electricity that lights us up had been turned off in him.

"Can you come back?" I asked him, "Because I miss you." It's not enough to have a person physically there if they're not there emotionally.

He looked at me with a blank look. "I'm right here," he said, though of course he wasn't.

And then, just like that, the blank façade crumpled right in front of me. He didn't say anything, but the animation slowly returned to his face, as if he were waking up. Like a switch had been turned on.

He didn't have to say anything. I could see he was coming back. I was never so glad to see someone.

"I've been right here," he said, when I told him I was glad to see him come back.

"No, you weren't. You weren't there at all."

"Oh. I thought I was here."

Could he really not tell? Was he so disconnected from his true self that he didn't know? It didn't really matter because he was back, and this was just another incident in a life filled with incidents. His returns from that empty place always made me giddy with relief, and it was contagious. No wonder we laughed so much, there was always something to celebrate because there so many instances of him fading away like that and coming back again. This happened more often later on than it did earlier in his illness.

When it became really difficult for me to manage two households, and when Stew didn't move away, we tried to rent a house so I could have him under the same roof again. The reasons we'd moved to separate apartments no longer existed, and looking after him from a distance was draining me. At least in the same house, I could see he was okay at night. And if he had issues at night, which was when he was likely to have them, it'd be much easier if we could just get together in the living room. We were truly just friends now, not recently separated and still raw from the betrayals we'd heaped on each other.

That, and it had become such an effort for me to keep his place current on bills, and mine too, and that's not even counting the money itself, but the effort to pay all the bills. Every day I spent hours taking care of Stew, and working, and I was so tired.

That, and I wanted a house. Honey wanted a house. She'd come to live with us when Stew and I lived in the apartment together, and I'd promised her that someday she'd have her own yard. I know, she was just a dog, but she was my dog. I wanted to be back in a house. How convenient if we could all be together. I'd become involved with Andrew, and he didn't mind. In fact, he was very supportive of my role in taking care of Stew. When Andrew and I went out together we often brought something back for Stew. Food, or dessert, or something.

Stew and I looked at houses and I wondered who was going to be convinced by our act. It's not an act, it's just us, but we're not your typical couple looking at houses. We're not a couple at all, not as I'm told it's currently defined, though we are a couple of people. Two friends — one mentally ill — looking for a house to rent. Of me I shall not comment because there is some perception that I too am mentally ill, but since the majority of opinions say I'm somewhat sane, I won't entertain the notion. Besides, it's difficult enough getting anything done with one mentally ill person in the bunch, much worse with two.

So I'm perfectly fine myself, thank you very much for asking.

And I wondered what people were thinking. It's human nature to judge, to form opinions about things which one does not know about, and for those who are unfamiliar with mental illness (though I do wonder how anyone these days can be unfamiliar with it, it appears to be everywhere) the propensity to step back when confronted with mental illness is strong. Why not? It's unfamiliar. On television, the mentally ill are always committing crimes and causing disturbances. Certainly there can't be a modicum of stability and safety with one of THEM hanging around.

I beg to differ, but I can do that later. No, wait, I'll do it now. Dealing with the mentally ill isn't that much different from dealing with anyone else, as long as one remembers who one is dealing with.
It is not in my nature to lie. So with potential landlords I am unfailingly honest.

"He's schizophrenic." If I don't say it myself, he will. He does not hide from it. "I look after him."

I'm looked at askance at times. Whatever. If being looked at askance is the worst thing that happens to me I'm in pretty good shape. And we need a house. I can no longer look after him in his apartment without going nuts myself. I know he shouldn't be out at night but he often is, at least to walk the dog, but I let the dog stay with him because she's good for him. I know that sometimes he needs someone close by, and on those rare occasions when he's needed middle of the night intervention it would be much easier if he weren't way over there. No one likes to be up and about at those hours. If I could just go downstairs, it would be much easier for me. I can no longer manage bill paying for two separate households. I can barely manage it for one. And it's not even the fact of the money, though that is in short supply, as much as it is the duplication of everything that must be paid. Making sure his household is in good working order, that things aren't falling down around him. Hard to do, it isn't always easy to get over there. That's silly, isn't it? It's not as if he's that far away.

Everything all together, this is what it comes down to. He needs a bit more supervision, and it will also make him feel a bit safer, a bit more secure, which can only be good for him.

We found a house that would work well. It had a separate apartment downstairs that Stew could live in, and a backyard, but when we told the landlord that Stew was mentally ill and I was his caretaker she backed off. She and her husband were Christian missionaries, and this rental property was their old house. They had a newer, bigger house, but didn't want to sell the old house outright.

I begged for the house. By this time, I had bad credit and a disabled ex-spouse who went everywhere with me. I wasn't the most appealing tenant. I wrote a long sob story of a letter, because by this time I had no dignity left. She relented, but said we could have the upstairs, and she was going to rent the downstairs out to someone else. That would mean no access to the backyard, unless we were to go out the front door and around the house to the back, which rather defeated the purpose of having a backyard, if you ask me. She also wanted me to buy her house a fence, and share appliances, which she wanted us to buy, with the downstairs tenant. We backed out, at which point she became irate and yelled at me.

On to the next house. We found an older house that had been redone. It was great inside. I loved the hardwood floors, and downstairs was a separate living area that Stew was happy with. We applied, but someone with better credit got it.

We looked and looked. We came up empty. It was a plan that would never come to anything at all, and I became frustrated. Who would rent to the crazy couple who weren't a couple? I just wanted what was best for us. And with no end in sight to the caretaking, being in the same residence seemed easier. I was ready for easier. Life had been so hard for so long.

But then Stew's parents broached the idea of him moving back home. By this time he was much more stable than he had been, and his visions were decreasing. They couldn't keep supporting him from a distance — it really wasn't fair to them, after all — and so he made the decision, reluctantly, to move back to California.

It wasn't that he didn't want to live with his parents, but he enjoyed being on his own. He felt that by moving back in with his parents at his age he was going backward, not forward. I told him it doesn't matter what other people say, that families do what they need to do to get through life, and that there was nothing wrong with living with his parents. That, and he loved the Pacific Northwest. He'd always wanted to get away from northern California, and to return to it was not what he'd envisioned. His life was in Washington.

But we packed him up, and I told him it was only temporary, that he could move back up later, and that nothing was forever.

Nothing is forever, except for those things that are forever. He put some of his things in storage, believing he'd be coming back up in a year or so, and he moved back to northern California.

CHAPTER 9

California is where our history together started, and it was to California he returned, alone, to live with his parents. We both talked about how it was just temporary, and someday he'd come back up north to live. He'd win his Social Security disability claim, eventually, and that would give him some income, but the best case scenario was that he would become self-sustaining. He worked at building an eBay business and was in the process of taking on commissions. He had potential.

By January of 2005, the psychosis was mostly absent, and his daily gloom wasn't as bad as it had been. The meds were working, as well as these things can, and he hadn't had hallucinations in months. He was still cutting pretty regularly, but overall doing better.

January 22, 2005
Journal Entry

I feel like I've failed, though I haven't. I have to remember that, don't I? He has to move away, back to California, to stay with his parents for awhile. He's packing right now, packing up his apartment, getting ready to put things in storage, to take what he needs on his "extended vacation" and leave the rest here.

And I will have the relief of knowing, late at night when he's having hallucinations, or when the demons visit, or when he's just overcome with the futility of survival in a world where his mind plays such tricks on him, that he's safe under his parents' roof, that he's not living alone. That he is not alone.

He feels he's too old to be living with his parents. I tell him that doesn't enter into it. Age and need are not related, age and where we should be at any particular place in our lives aren't necessarily connected, and for now this is the best solution.

I need time to get back on my feet. I'm just one person, and though I've kept him safe for several years, it's time for someone else to take a turn. A team of people, this time, people who don't have to work for a living anymore. I must work, I don't have the time, and I don't have the emotional resources to carry on like this indefinitely. Does anyone? Perhaps, I tell myself, if I were a better person, I would have managed it. But I'm not, I'm just who I am.

There's no reason why I can't do everything, is there? Other than the fact that I'm just one person, that is. Other than the fact that I'm stretched in all directions as far as I can go, and there is very little stretching left that I can do without breaking something. Something that I might need later. Like my mind. Or my health.

So he's preparing for his move, and he's managing it well. He's dealing with it well, especially considering how difficult change is for him. He's going to miss me, and he's going to miss Dog, so Dog is staying with him as much as possible before he goes. February 2nd. That's when he's supposed to go. I told him he must come back and visit now and then.

He'll be close to his best friend too, after he moves, to the best man who stood up at our wedding. His friend is glad to have him back. I'm glad too. That's three whole people he has down there for support, instead of just one.

Instead of just me.

I tell him he'll do fine, and he will. I will do fine also. Will I still have an identity when he's gone? I've invested so much of myself into his care but I know that it's not me, that there is much more to me than that, and I will be fine. I have my life here, I have my love, I have me. We'll communicate frequently, I'm sure. I've told him to keep his cell phone, so he can call me anytime. We still have the computer to talk through. I want to make it clear that he's not being abandoned, or sent away because I've suddenly decided to concentrate on my new relationship, but that this is what is best for everyone. It will alleviate my stress knowing that he is not living alone.

Living alone is not working for him right now, though he wanted it so much and tried so hard. He may have thought it was working for him, but he doesn't pay his bills, he doesn't clean up after himself, usually. He forgets to do the things that must be done on a regular basis when one is a functioning member of society. He lives in his own little world. He has improved so much though. His self-awareness is quite good. Sometimes too good. Sometimes knowing your mind has betrayed you is worse than not knowing. I want him to find his place, and I think he needs his independence from me to learn what he's capable of.

Am I rationalizing? Am I saying he needs this or that to make myself feel better about having failed? I don't think so. I think I am right. Some might say he'll then be dependent on others, but it's a different dynamic, and he'll have more incentive to find his own way.

It's time. I have a life I must concentrate on right now, a very significant relationship, and to work at getting back on my feet. To get upright again.

So here we go.

April 2, 2005
Journal Entry

We've slacked off on our reporting. In Borderland, things are quiet. Everyone is striving for normalcy, though that is more a state of mind than anything else.

Stew is in California, and we've both had to relearn how to do things. I, for example, can now, on the days I'm not scheduled to meet with clients, stay in my office (aka home) all day and work, and not see any other people. In the morning my domestic partner is here, and at night. In between, I'm responsible for no one besides myself. And the dog. And various clients in various stages of panic, but there are entire days when even they are all quiet. They all think I'm working on their problems is why, and they know that to leave me alone means I can, perhaps, work faster. I try to bunch my client visits together, so I can spend big blocks of time on one project or another, and other big blocks of time going here and there. Yesterday, Friday, April 1, I saw four clients, one of them a new one, and didn't get home until 9 pm.

Anyway, this isn't about me.

This is about our friend Stew. He's doing pretty well. Considering.

Considering, that is, that he's in an area where the options for receiving help are severely limited. One therapist doesn't believe in the borderline diagnosis. One doesn't treat people who self-harm. (But who then gave Stew another appointment, and about the self-harm issue said, "Just don't do it anymore." Aw gee, why didn't anyone else think of that?) Another therapist he had an appointment with was found to have lost his license "back East," for unspecified reasons. Stew decided not to go to that one. The community mental health office isn't quite sure what to do with him. He's an oddity, as one evaluator there told him. He doesn't use drugs, he doesn't drink, he's highly intelligent, and he has all his teeth. She's more used to dealing with what is typically known as the "dregs of society." That's nice that they have a category for them.

So they put him in day camp. Three days a week. To learn basic social skills, apparently. Sigh. He said it felt like kindergarten. He missed quite a few of the days for various reasons. I don't blame him. They envision for him some sort of perhaps low-level job where he can be a drone.

He wants to go back to school and study statistics some more. He wants to be an actuary. He wants to do more writing. He's checking into taking classes. He's signed up for an online writing class with the local college. He's selling things on eBay. He's DOING THINGS.

He feels isolated at times. He feels alone. He has his parents, he has me, but it's so easy to lose touch with friends. He hasn't heard from his best friend in several weeks. I told him today to give him a call, that it's okay. I told him to talk to another old friend he sees around town, that it's okay. He forgets that. He thinks no one wants to hang around with him, that people avoid him. It's not true of course. People like him, they just get wrapped up in their own lives. We all do. It is true that some people don't know how to respond, and can't deal with it, but that's not his fault. I tell him that. He's a likable guy. He just needs more contact with more people.

He's cut a few times since he moved to California. The first time his mother dealt with it well. I'd told her it wasn't a big deal, he cleans up after himself, usually it helps him feel a bit better (personally, I think this method of dealing is better than drinking or drugs, both very common for people like him), and not to panic about it. I talk or chat online with him daily, and with his mother. I reassure her, when she doesn't know what to do.

One day I chatted with her while I chatted with him at the same time, relaying information back and forth on the situation, how he was, and what he was feeling. They were in the same house, but he didn't know how to tell her what he was feeling without upsetting her. I am still the universal translator.

Sometimes I can't tell how he is without hearing his voice, so I call him. I do phone counseling. I make him laugh. I tell him amusing stories about the Killing Machine (also known as Honey.) Sometimes, when I'm down because I doubt myself, he helps me. He talks to me sternly, he tells me how ridiculous I am, and he's right.

I'm very proud of him. Like all of us, he's a work in progress, and the important thing is that he is working on it. That's what matters: He hasn't given up, he doesn't let his illness consume him.

———

Life since Moving Back to California
By Stew

May, 2005

It wasn't entirely unexpected. My parents only had so much money, and I knew that over the past year they'd given Monique and me quite a lot. And I knew my mom was getting more worried about me. So it wasn't a big surprise when they said, "How about if you move on back to California for a little while?"

And it wasn't that California is a bad place to live. It's just that Yuba City is a horrendous place to live. I once told Jake that the only way I'd move back to California is in a pine box. I once told somebody else that I'd rather be homeless in Seattle than in a nice home in Yuba City. But as Tim says, "They always come back." (So far, Tim hasn't. Lucky bastard.)

Yuba City, California — for those of you who aren't acquainted with it — is not quite the middle of nowhere, but you can see it from there. It's forty miles north of Sacramento, forty miles south of Chico, ninety miles west of Reno, and ninety miles northeast of San Francisco. Yuba City is a little farm town, whose little farm-town days are numbered, but the city "fathers" are going kicking and screaming.

Fortunately, in the seven years I've been gone, some of the farmers saw the writing on the wall, and sold their land to developers, and now Yuba City, much to the chagrin of the local residents, has become a bedroom community to Sacramento. That can only be a good thing. You see, Yuba City and the surrounding area have about an eighteen percent unemployment rate (as high as twenty-five percent in neighboring Colusa County.) The people coming in and buying these new houses actually have some money because they work in Sacramento, and they are starting to do some of their shopping in Yuba City. Thus a little bit more money is coming into the area. Yuba City now has two Starbucks and a Home Depot!

And here's the clincher: I think Yuba City is a pit, and so do some major financial magazines. In 1985, Rand McNally first listed the Yuba City area as the worst place to live in their *Places Rated Almanac,* a dishonor that has been awarded several times in the past twenty years by them and also by *Money* magazine. It's not just my opinion that Yuba City is a dump; it's the opinion of well-educated researchers. For the population, the crime rate is out of control. There's a spot not twenty minutes away that's known as the crystal meth capital of the state, if not the country.

Oh, and get this: When I was talking to the local mental health people, I was listed as a rarity, because I'm one of the few males they've seen who doesn't have a drug or alcohol problem, or has never been convicted of a felony. Classy place.

This tirade about Yuba City is only the beginning. I knew this stuff before I moved back. Now I know it's one of the worst places to live if you have a mental illness. There are very few mental health practitioners in town, and those that are in town are living in the dark ages.

The first doctor I tried to see — a psychiatrist — wouldn't have anything to do with cutters. He explained to me that cutting is beyond the level of involvement that he wants to get into. That he "is not adequately prepared to deal with it." His suggestion: When you feel like cutting, go to the ER. A few times of dealing with ER, you'll learn that cutting takes too much effort, time, and money to be an effective coping mechanism. You know what happens when this cutter goes to the ER? He gets more anxious, and he finds whatever tools he can to cut himself with, including his own fingernails.

A psychiatrist who doesn't deal with cutters? Isn't that like a dermatologist who doesn't deal with rashes? What's the guy do all day? As the gal at the local mental health department said, "Seventy-five percent of our clients are cutters." Wouldn't want to get our hands dirty dealing with real mental health issues, do we?

The next guy I saw was almost as bad. He was a psychologist. I've learned over the years that psychologist can mean a lot of different things, from somebody who does therapy (like Dr. Geiger) or somebody who just pretends to know a lot about psychological issues. Maybe they really do know a lot about psychological issues, they probably are dealing with some themselves. But this guy was a real huckster. His brand of psychology had me singing to myself. Literally! He said the singing disrupts mental pathways and I wouldn't feel so compulsive or obsessive. You know what one of the things I'm obsessive and compulsive about? Song lyrics. Some people get a song stuck in their head for a few days, while I get entire orchestras stuck in my head for weeks at a time. It becomes the pervasive thought for long stretches of time. Every single note, over and over again until I'm ready to scream. If I actually knew something about music, I'd make handy use of this. But I can't tell a flat C to a straight A. If there is such a thing.

He also wanted me to go on the South Beach Diet. All my emotional and psychological troubles are because I eat too many carbohydrates. Uh huh. That would be a great epitaph to use on my gravestone, never mind that I'd slit my own throat because of the pure morose I feel most days. Great, now on top of everything I feel guilty about, I have to feel guilty about cheating on my diet.

Do these people even think about what they're telling me?

And these two numbskulls were the ones that I was referred to by other doctors in the area. No wonder the community is at eighteen percent unemployment. People who live here are depressed because they can't get any help for their depression.

Fortunately (he said ironically) there is a mental health facility run by the county in this area. Sutter-Yuba Mental Health (named after the counties they help, Sutter County and Yuba County. The meth capital of the nation is in Yuba. Yuba City is in Sutter. Yeah, I know.)

I will say this for Sutter-Yuba Mental Health: They try hard. I'm sure they're underfunded and understaffed. I'm sure they are the red-headed stepchild of governmental departments. But at least the workers I've seen try hard. They may not know what to do, or how to do it, but they work within the constraints they have.

See, I'm literally too smart for my own good. If I was just an average every-day run-of-the-mill narcotic- or alcohol-obsessed person with a mental illness then filling me full of meds and letting me lie around in a catatonic state would work well. Some days, most days, I wish I was that type of person. (Lots more help out there for the narcotic- and alcohol-obsessed people.) But I'm too self-aware. I know there's a better life out there. Well, at least I see other people with better lives, and I think, "Why can't that be me?"

So fitting me into something is more difficult. I tried Sutter-Yuba Mental Health's adult day treatment program. And that's fine for the bulk of the people they are trying to help. It's 9 am-to-2 pm and you come in and learn a variety of things, like how to get along with people and how to dress for success. Sometimes we just sit and make "Happy St. Patrick's Day" cards for the other inmates, er, patients. All in all, it's a kindergarten-like environment for adults. Which is fine. But I don't need to be sitting next to guy who can barely keep his eyes open, or a girl who repeatedly wants to know when nap time is (it's at 1:30, every day.) Or the guy with Tourette's syndrome.

I need to be with people like me. Reasonably intelligent folk whose brains just won't allow them to be in polite society for too long. There are a few of us out there. I met them at the depression support group in Washington. Problem is: They were too depressing. (And most of them were alcohol- or narcotic-obsessed.)

The people at this day program, for the most part, I don't think many of them could have told you where they were. Few of them could carry on a conversation that I found to be coherent. (And most of those conversations were about motorcycles or sports). I'm not looking to join a Mensa group, but come on! There must be depressed and anxiety-ridden people who can talk about books, movies, restaurants, or, God forbid, a newspaper headline.

Although, I must admit, through Sutter-Yuba Mental Health, I do think I found one of the better psychiatrists I've had. Dr. Randhawa. I don't know what he's doing here in Yuba City, he could easily be working in Sacramento or San Francisco, but God bless, he's here. As you can tell by his name, he's Indian. From India. He talks fast and has a bit of an accent, but I can understand most of what he says. He's got a sense of humor, too, which is refreshing. He once told me that his colleagues have told him that he has his turban wrapped too tight. He also knows my lawyer.

Ah yes, my lawyer. Yuba City does seem to have its fair share of lawyers. I'm not sure what to make of that, but there it is. I need a lawyer to go after Social inSecurity.

See, it seems that many people with my conditions (and some not quite to my extent) get money from the government because they are disabled. Social inSecurity seems to think I'm still able to work. They agree that there may be some discomfort and pain working in an office environment, but they think I should be working as a dishwasher.

I worked as a dishwasher for about four months one time. I probably felt more stress on that job than I did at Health Care Subsidiary. Working alongside a hot machine, carrying loads of dishes, careful not to drop any stray food item into the vat of pancake batter that was located next to the dishwashing station, having somebody with 50 IQ points fewer than me barking orders at me like I was her slave. And then there was the guy who was recently released from Folsom Prison for manslaughter. Nope. No stress there. Oh, and let's use some common sense: I like to cut my arms with a kitchen knife when I become stressed or irritated. Dishwashing at a diner? Easy access to knives and other sharp implements. That extra special seasoning in tonight's gravy? Oh, that's the blood, sweat, and tears from our very own mentally-distressed dishwasher. C'mon people, get a clue.

———

Stew won his disability claim. It went all the way to a judge, who looked at the paperwork and said, "Why did this have to come all this way?" (And then the judge told Stew and his lawyer how to make really good bran muffins.) Stew received back benefits. He had Medicaid. He could now receive medical care with the county. I was still struggling to get back on my feet, but at least one of us was in good shape financially. There's no financial compensation for the caretaker, of course. We've got to figure that out ourselves.

His parents had rented an office space for him, someplace he could go to work on things. He was working as an eBay assistant, getting the occasional commission, and working on our book. He wanted people to know what it was like to deal with this illness. He was able to see his friends, and we still kept in touch on a daily basis, through emails and chat and phone calls. When he was unsure about something, he'd run it by me. He was still scared of trying things. What if he went out with the guys but got sick? I'd tell him to go ahead and give it a try, and if he couldn't stay, they'd understand. I told him there was nothing wrong with having to leave early, that trying is the important thing. I didn't want him to give up.

He had good times and bad times, but mostly he had better times. He took scriptwriting courses and collaborated with other writers. He attempted a bit of dating, but didn't make a lot of progress. Most of the people he talked to were online, since that was the safest environment for him.

It would be an understatement to say we kept in touch. We messaged most every day, and talked on the phone, and we celebrated every accomplishment, both his and mine.

When Andrew and I moved into a place big enough for two and my office (and his, it would turn out), Stew drove up and helped us. He wasn't well, physically, but I told him he didn't have to help with the actual moving. He took on the task of setting up my computer and did what he could to help. In 2006, Andrew and I took a vacation, and Stew came up again to house-sit for us.

Andrew and I had another dog by then in addition to Honey. Ash was still a puppy, a high-energy lab blue heeler mix, and so we put him in the kennel while we were gone. Sometimes Ash was more than we could stand sometimes, and we knew he'd drive Stew crazy.

This was one of those surreal times. For some reason I don't remember, I flew out a day before Andrew, and left Stew and Andrew at home in the apartment Andrew and I shared. They ate out together, and they got along just fine. The next day Andrew flew out, and Stew looked after Honey and the apartment.

That was a big accomplishment for him. He could drive back and forth from California to Seattle, and he could be on his own, and he was fine.

So 2006 was a good year, but Stew wasn't feeling well. Still, he had many plans for the future, once he got his health under control. I was so proud of him, and he was such a good friend to both Andrew and me. He'd fought his illness so well.

When Andrew and I went anywhere we'd bring Stew something back. Andrew was often the instigator. He knew Stew was like a younger brother to me, and he was so awesome about accepting Stew as part of my life.

Stew was sick for a very long time. Not just the mental illness sort of sick, but physically. He'd had the peptic ulcer, and he'd had lots of digestive issues, and after he moved to California he still had them, and they got worse.

And when his digestive problems only worsened they tested him for everything they could think of — but not for what he had — until they ran out of other options. Each new diagnosis would turn out to be wrong, and they'd try another.

He threw up a lot. While he was more stable mentally than he'd been in years, physically he was more of a wreck than ever. He'd call me with each new diagnosis, hopeful that this would be the one, and that they would fix it and he could get on with his life. His paranoia was mostly gone, he still had problems with crowds and people and he couldn't see well at night, but he wasn't hallucinating, he didn't have the demons stalking him anymore, and there was light at the end of the tunnel.

In May of 2007, Andrew and I married. Stew and his parents came up to our wedding. Stew wasn't feeling well at the wedding, but I hoped he'd be able to stay for the reception. I had a room set aside for him to escape to, but after the ceremony he said he had to go, he wasn't feeling well at all and he couldn't deal with the crush of people. On the way back to California, he and his parents stopped off at the storage unit and emptied it of his belongings. This made me sad. How could I keep pretending he'd move back up when all his things were gone? I knew how much he hated the summers in California.

He was doing well, if only he weren't so physically sick.

I remember the day he called me with the final, and correct, diagnosis, just a couple of months after the wedding. I was working for a company, a short-lived experiment when they made me an offer I couldn't refuse. After years of instability, I couldn't refuse the opportunity of stability. So I was at work, in the office, when he called on my cell phone. I always answered his calls if there were any way I could.

"They finally know what's wrong me," he said.

"What?"

"It's cancer," he said. "And it's terminal."

What can anyone say to that?

He told me that they might be able to delay it for years, that with chemo perhaps it wouldn't advance too quickly. It had started in his colon, and they might have been able to stop it if they'd found it then, but they hadn't found it before it'd spread to his liver, and there wasn't anything they could do except perhaps give him more time.

What's the definition of "more time?" How much time can you give the dying when they know they're dying? We're all dying, and while the reality is we can go anytime, it's another matter altogether to being told you're dying. Suddenly there's a limit, and it's no longer an unforeseeable future event, but a real possibility, perhaps sooner rather than later. Probably sooner rather than later, in fact.

He was in the hospital for seventeen days, and he looked forward to returning home to attempt to take up a life-in-waiting, and to make the best of it.

At first the chemo went well. At first Stew thought he might have more time, and he talked about returning to school if the cancer was going to take its time killing him.

He went into the hospital when he had a blockage, and then he came out, and he started getting worse.

Andrew and I made plans to spend Christmas with Stew and his parents, though we hoped he'd have years left. But we didn't know, so we planned for the worst.

We drove down a couple of days before Christmas in 2007. We stayed at a local hotel, and Stew looked as if he were feeling okay. He had a pump for his chemo, but he got around okay, and the three of us drove around and went to look at the house Stew and I had lived in before we'd moved north, the big house on the hill I'd lost to foreclosure when I couldn't afford it. The new owners had, of course, ruined it. Don't they always? Then Stew took us to his office and showed us around. One of my favorite pictures is one Andrew took of Stew and me there.

At the time, it looked as if he might continue on for a good long while. He seemed to be more at peace than I'd seen him for quite some time. Perhaps because he knew that there would eventually be an end to his pain, perhaps it was because the demons no longer showed up to terrorize him. His mental status since his diagnosis had been remarkably better, I thought.

"Since it looks like it won't kill me right away, I might as well do something useful," he said to me.

After Christmas told him I'd come back in a few months to visit.

He'd borne the diagnosis fairly well, considering. He seemed to come to a sort of peace with it, and I believe he was not altogether unhappy about the prospect of his pain — both mental and physical — someday coming to an end. His life hadn't been easy for years, and he now had the prospect of peace to look forward to. He bore his diagnosis with grace.

———

Email to Our Writing Group
By Stew

November 13, 2007

I had an oncologist appointment and he said, "Things are looking pretty good. Let's put you on another medication!"

I said "Fine."

He said, "There are some side effects with this one."

"Okay. Like what?"

"Nose bleeds."

I said, "Annoying but tolerable."

"It can raise your blood pressure."

"I've lowered it significantly over the past few months, a few points north won't hurt me."

He nodded and said (damn I can't remember the exact word he used), "It can cause a [tear] in your bowels."

I said, "That doesn't sound good."

He said, "Don't worry. It only affects five percent of the people who take this drug who already had colon surgery."

I said, "Okay, go on."

"Blood clots. Do you have a history of blood clots?"

I said, "No. What would blood clots do?"

"If they traveled to your heart, you'd experience cardiac complications."

I said, "That doesn't sound pleasant at all."

He said, "Don't worry. It only affects five percent of the people who take this drug who already have a history of blood clots."

I said, "Okay. Go on."

He said, "Death."

"That's a pretty dramatic side effect, don't you think?"

He said, "Don't worry; it only affects five percent of the people who have been dead before."

I said, "What a wonder drug."

So. The first time you use this medication (given via IV, so it's given in conjunction with the chemo meds), they give it to you over the course of ninety minutes.

"Slow for safety," the nurse said. You've got to worry about any drug that they need to wear special thicker gloves for. This medication is a liquid, surrounded in plastic bag, inside another plastic bag when they get

it from the pharmacy. But still the nurses have to wear special thicker purple hazmat gloves when transporting it from the pharmacy to the patient. But the patient doesn't get to wear anything when this stuff goes straight into the chest (or arm.)

And they have to take your blood pressure every fifteen minutes. And they come around every twenty minutes or so, to check that you're still alive.

On the bright side: If you do live, the second session with this drug is only sixty minutes. And if you survive that one, then it goes down to thirty minutes.

What does this drug do? It kills off the blood vessels feeding the tumors. How does it know which blood vessels to kill off? The handout I got today said, "Researchers are still investigating how [this drug] works, but it appears to kill off just those blood vessels related to the tumor."

STILL INVESTIGATING? APPEARS? Is this the best the scientific community can do? Why are they still investigating? Didn't they create this drug with the mindset that it would kill off the bad blood vessels?

Sheesh...

How was your day?

Our chats and emails, as written, sound like they might have been between illiterates raised without formal education or the willingness to try to sound like we knew how to use the English language. But it's a ruse: Part shortcut language because of our shared history, part because when one does countless chats and emails, saving every keystroke counts. I could say that was the only reason, but it's not. It was just something we did. It's cleaned up a little, here.

November 26, 2007

Stew: Hulllo?

Monique: Hi!

Stew: How you?

Monique: I fine, how you?

Stew: Angry, sad, depressed.

Monique: Oh, I sorry! Can I help?

Stew: I don't think so.

Monique: What's wrong?

Stew: Both feet hurt, for one thing. I don't want to get chemo anymore. I'm constantly tired. I can't do anything, etc.

Monique: Oh. Yeah. Of course you're angry, sad and depressed. It's not unexpected. Why not get chemo anymore?

Stew: I dunno. I hate sitting there for four or five hours. It's boring. LOL. Then I get all tired for a week afterwards.

Monique: LOL. Yeah, I'm sure it is boring. But you seem to be feeling a lot better with it than you were before.

Stew: Yeah. Not as nauseated. I dunno. I guess I'm just grumpy today.

Monique: Well, duh. It's a Monday after a holiday. Everyone's grumpy. Everyone's like, "Hey! What happened? How'd it get to be MONDAY again?"

Stew: Oh.

Monique: I was grumpy when I woke up. The immersion back into reality sucks. LOL.

Stew: LOL.

Monique: That's the problem with holidays. Even if you don't do much for them, they're STILL holidays, so in our minds they're still SPECIAL. Then they end. And we all look around us, stunned, and say, "What happened? Where'd it go?"

Stew: What happened? Where'd it go?

Monique: Exactly! Where did it go? It was just here, dammit! Now it's gone! Damn holidays. Always running off on us. Fickle, those holidays.

Stew: And it's too damn sunny outside.

[And much later, after we'd discussed the dogs, the weather, the cancer, all while avoiding politics, Stew changed the subject.]

Stew: I'm leaving now for the great unknown.

Monique: Your recliner?

Stew: For awhile. Then I have to go visit vampires.

Monique: Aha! Vampires! Tell them I said hi!

Stew: Okay.

Monique: Later, I shall try my foolproof grump aversion therapy.

Stew: Okay.

Monique: As soon as I figure out what it is. You be first to know though!

Stew: Oh good! Talk to ya later!

He was grumpy a lot, and it was still my mission to help, and so whenever he was up for it I'd chat with him. We'd go off and on all day, and I think he liked knowing I was usually just a few keystrokes away.

Email from Stew, December 30, 2007

I'm on a new keyboard now. I'm not sure how I like it yet, since this is the first thing I ever typed on it. And it just popped up a help screen, like it's trying to be helpful or something. Hmmm.

As I said, I'm much better today. I'm going to go back to school this summer or fall. I told Mom and Dad, "Since it doesn't look like the cancer's gonna kill me quickly, I should probably plan on doing something." So, I'm thinking about going to University of Phoenix online and getting my MBA. I think that would be the most prudent move, but I like the idea of going to a real school (Sac or Chico State) and getting a degree in economics. But the commute to and from Sac would be hard. Chico is not so bad, but most of the classes I need are offered at night, and you know me and night driving. Any thoughts you have would be appreciated.

So, I guess I like this new keyboard. I can type pretty fast on it. Hope all is well. Email me when you can.

Talk later. Have good time with in-laws. Are you off tomorrow?

Email from Stew. December 31, 2007

Hey. I just received the EOB for my hospital stay and my chemo. It's about $100,000. It's $15,000 each time I have chemo. Wow, I'm expensive.

Reply: *You're expensive but you're worth it! Every freakin' cent of it!*

Reply*: Yes! I know! :)*

Chat. March 4, 2008

Stew: I'm dying.

Monique: What?

Stew: This pain is killing me.

Monique: Oh baby, I'm so sorry.

Stew: I see doctor at 10:30 or so. Hopefully he'll give me something for pain.

Monique: Yes, I would certainly hope so! Demand relief!

Stew: Morphine.

Monique: Yes, if that's what helps.

Stew: How you?

Monique: Oh, I fine.

Stew: Good.

Monique: I just worried about you.

Stew: Yeah.

Monique: I want you to feel better.

Stew: Yeah.

Monique: Yeah.

Stew: Sigh.

Monique: Sigh. We miss you.

Stew: We miss you too. I'm ready to stab myself in the gut.

Monique: Yeah, I'm thinking that would be a bad idea.

Stew: Yeah.

Monique: Mom might be upset about it too.

Stew: Yeah, probably.

Monique: And dad. And I'm not sure it would really help.

Stew: I don't think it would hurt though. Or maybe it might.

Monique: Yeah, it might hurt a little. It might be a different pain though.

Stew: A different pain would be nice.

Monique: Well, it would be a change of pace, anyway. Which does not mean I'm advocating it!

Stew: I know.

Monique: Just wanted to make sure that was clear.

Stew: Yes. So sleepy.

Monique: No time for nap before doctor, huh? Maybe doctor give you something for pain and you can come home and take nice nap.

Stew: I hope so.

Monique: Yeah, me too. Want me to call him? I tell him myself!

Stew: Okay.

Monique: I say, GIVE HIM SOMETHING THAT WORKS!

Stew: Yes.

Monique: I can be quite annoying when aggravated.

Chat March 13, 2008.

Stew: Goood morning?

Monique: Hi!

Stew: Hiya

Monique: How's you?

Stew: Oh, suddenly in a lot of pain, but not too bad.

Monique: Yikes! Belly? Shoulder? Psyche?

Stew: Belly.

Monique: Oh. More pain meds? Any word on when new chemo starts?

Stew: I'll take some in a few minutes. New chemo starts Wednesday.

Monique: Oh good.

Stew: It takes a full-time secretary to keep me on schedule.

An email I wrote to a friend. May 7, 2008

It sucks. And it doesn't suck. I'm of two minds, naturally.

Stew had chemo today, and while he was there waiting the social worker talked to him. She told him that unless they find the "right" chemo, he has one to two months left. His liver is shot. None of this is a surprise. Since they've been unable to find the right chemo so far, or any effective treatment, I rather doubt they're suddenly going to come up with something.

We talked about it for awhile, about how he gets to escape and be at peace, while the rest of us are stuck here in this place that can be so messy and painful.

We talked about how he's not afraid of death, he's afraid of the dying part. We talked about how much we'll miss him, and him us, and we laughed about how he's going to haunt me. We talked about how even when he's gone he'll still be here with us anyway.

We talked about how he's going to send messages. No doubt it will have something to do with bears. I told him how some of us hear from those who've passed on.

We talked about hospice. I told him what I know about it, which, since I've been in orientation to be a volunteer this week, is more than I knew last week. I'll recommend it, even if he doesn't think he needs it, because they're just there to help, and even if he doesn't need it, it will help his parents.

We talked about how tired he is. His thirties have been mostly filled with pain of one kind or another, after all. I told him that the good die young, so I'll live forever. And he laughed.

He's more up than he has been lately because now he has something, a goal. It's not going to be several more years of agony and helplessness. It's a chance to move on to something better. It's just getting past the dying part that concerns him.

We talked about my hotel when I come down there in a few weeks. I told him we'd probably use some of our Hilton points. He said he wanted to pay for a night. I told him that wasn't necessary, and he said, "What else am I going to do with my money?" And we laughed.

Then he went to eat the hamburger from In'N'Out his dad had gotten him. At this stage he asks for whatever he feels like eating and they get it for him because why the hell not? He's going to throw up ANYWAY. He may as well eat what he wants.

We talked about how the doctor sent the social worker in with that special bit of news and the next step is to talk to the doctor, which won't be until Tuesday, and I said, "What the? They tell you that, and then tell you to wait until Tuesday to talk to the doctor?"

And now he's back online chatting with me again and positively, I swear, giddy with relief. He typed: "bipolar disorder, depression, schizophrenia, cancer, cutting, two months to live, and what hurts the most right now? A hang nail."

He'll never stop making me laugh.

One of our last chats.

Monique: Yay! Someone said something nice about you today.

Stew: Who? What?

Monique: "He is such a beautiful soul, Monique. He probably has no idea how much he has touched our hearts over the years, but his courage, faith, and persistence are, and have been, an inspiration. He's made lots of people love him just by being who he is.

I have Stew on the prayer list at church and if you think he'd like it, I'll have a mass said for him. Or two. Or twenty.

If it's okay, I'd like to send this to the prayer group. They have been praying for you guys for some time. Let me know if it's okay."

Linda in New York.

Stew: Cool. Coool.

Monique: Cool.

Stew: You have nice friends.

Monique: And so do you. My friends are your friends.

––––––

Email from Stew's Mom. May 13, 2008

> *Stewart went to the doctor today. It looks like the liver is shrinking, but Stew asked that chemo be stopped for awhile. The side effects of the new drugs he is taking are worse than the cancer right now.*
>
> *Since coming home from the hospital last month, he has lost another forty-nine pounds. And Erbitux causes a terrible case of acne on his scalp. It itches and he has scratched his head so much that the hair is coming out in clumps and it is sore and red, and bleeds.*

He is still having lots of vomiting and that is with taking four different kinds of anti-nausea meds. From the nausea his potassium and magnesium levels are off and he has to have IVs for that.

He is very weak and sleeps most of the time. Since it is Stewart's choice to go off chemo the doctor said to see what happens when he is off for four or five months.

Hopefully he will get some strength back so he can get around more.

Of course, no matter what happens, he has less than a year to live. At least it will be on his terms. So far he is not in any real pain except for his scalp. We have discussed hospice but the doctor does not think he is ready for that just yet.

We have talked about his memorial service and what to have. I suggested plates of broccoli and bananas (the two foods he will not eat.) He actually seems better tonight. I think that knowing he will not have chemo tomorrow is helping.

He will still see the doctor and have blood tests every week to watch the potassium and magnesium. If they are low he will get those drugs in IVs. And he will go back if he gets dehydrated.

All we can do now is watch and wait. He wants to drive but until the vomiting stops we don't want him out in a car by himself.

Has been an up and down day. Let's see what tomorrow brings.

May 13, 2008
Journal Entry

The chemo merry-go-round may still be spinning, but Stew is no longer on it. He has made his decision, and it wasn't hard for him at all. When I spoke with him he sounded better than he had in days, more cheerful, more at peace, more ready for his next adventure, because he can see that there will be a next adventure coming up, that it's not going to be an eternity of being sick and in pain, weekly chemo and tests and procedures and on and on for as long as the mind can see, which is quite a bit farther than the eye can see.

I was at the beach two weekends ago. It was slightly overcast, and extremely windy, and looking up the coast I thought I could see for miles and miles. The ocean played tricks on my eyes, and I looked up the beach, to the north, and saw more beach, and more beach, and on and on, and I thought that if I were to walk on and on for days I'd still be walking along that beach, and I'd still be heading north, and there'd be no end to it. That's how it looked to me, from where I stood. It would never end, this beach, and I could never get to the end of it, no matter how far I walked.

I imagine — though I don't know — that he's been feeling the same way. An endless walk down a blustery beach of cancer and chemo that looks like it will never end, and it'll go on forever and ever, like some sort of purgatory on earth, with his life itself dwindling, but with the purgatory encasing his body and his spirit, an eternity of being stuck there with no end in sight. The end of chemo ends that cycle, and opens new doors.

He thinks he's putting others through so much, his parents especially, they're with him and attending to his every need. His every want. Since he throws up anything he eats, all pretense of giving him what he should eat has been dismissed. If he has a craving for an In'N'Out burger and fries, they get it for him. He wants beans and rice from his favorite Mexican place, they go get it. His appetite has been so small that anything he wants is considered good, and why not?

I've told him he's putting no one through anything, that everyone is doing what they want to do, and there are no easy solutions to this. He cannot disappear, as if he's never been, and make this easier for anyone, even himself. It's a process that he must go through, as we all go through our own processes. I've told him to let people take care of him, and to ask for what he needs and wants, and that we just want to help, and he has to let us. It's not his choice, nor ours, it is what it is, and we'll do what we can while he does what he must.

I know the times he has seemed happiest — even giddy even with relief — are when he has seen that there will be an end to this, even knowing what that end is.

A new adventure, time for a new game plan. The only certainties in life are those we all deal with. Life. Change. Death. We can be certain only of those, and while we each travel alone, we share those things with every other person, and so we are never truly alone.

Email from Stew
May 16, 2008

> *What'cha doing asleep at 2:30 in the morning? I've been up for an hour throwing up every fifteen minutes. Nobody to talk to makes me bored.*

> *Talk to you in a few hours.*

I planned on going down to visit Stew at the end of May, and we talked about what we'd do when I got there. Andrew was going to stay home, and I told Stew we'd go to the movies, something he hadn't done in quite a while.

He'd been in the hospital for a few days with an obstruction, and the time there was torturous for him. He said he didn't want to go back to the hospital, and he never did.

He did have chemo regularly, and I think he enjoyed it, as much as a person can. They'd order him lunch, and he'd watch recorded TV or movies, though usually he didn't have much of an attention span. He just couldn't do much for very long.

But he kept getting worse. He'd often fall asleep while sitting at his computer while we were chatting. He'd type something, and then I'd respond, but nothing. His scalp had started bleeding, and it became loose, as if it could slide right off his head. He was still throwing up every day. He'd made the decision to stop the chemo when the doctors said it wasn't working.

What kind of decision is that to have to make?

He spent most of his time dozing.

His mom called me one day and said he was asking for me, and suddenly waiting to go down to California was no longer an option. I got on a plane the next morning.

His mom and the next-door neighbor picked me up at the airport. Stew was never left alone now, and his dad was at home with him. When I walked in the house, Stew was sitting in the living room, in the recliner that was his, and I went to him and knelt next to him, and I held his hand. He smiled at me weakly, and he seemed to glow from the inside out, like a holy man. His scalp was healing, so he had scabs all over his head. And he'd lost so much weight, though he was still big. And incredibly weak. When his dad helped him to the restroom it was a difficult task.

My Stew was using a walker.

His hospital bed was in his room, and after that first day that's where he stayed. A final trip to the bathroom in the middle of the night was the last time he would attempt to get up. He slid off the bed, and between the three of us we couldn't get him back in bed, so we called the fire department, and they came and put him back in bed in the middle of the night.

For hours each day I sat by his side, talking to him if he were awake, holding his hand, and he'd still attempt jokes. Sometimes he'd look off as if he could see into the future, and several times he said something to the empty space that indicated he could see something we could not. Perhaps he could.

I've often wondered if it were possible that his condition — the mental one — made it possible for him to see things the rest of us couldn't. Perhaps it wasn't hallucinating so much as seeing things that most of us aren't attuned to. Fanciful thoughts, sure. But no more unreasonable than many others that are widely accepted.

For nine days his parents and I sat by his bedside, talking to him, being with him, and making him comfortable. Whatever he asked for, he got. Although he managed only a few sips of even his favorite drinks and smoothies and then he'd throw up again.

Since he threw up so often, the only reliable method of getting medication into him was to use topical morphine, and his father carefully rubbed it into his arm several times a day. His other medications, the ones for his mental illness, were no longer used. It was too difficult to get them down, so perhaps part of his hallucinating, if he was, could be attributed to that.

He was mostly there, though, during those last few days. We talked about all we'd been through together, and he worried about getting this wrong, too. As if dying were yet another test that he'd have to pass. So many times he fell asleep, hoping it was the last time, only to awaken later and find himself still there, in his bed. So he asked me, "What if I don't know how? What if I can't do it right?"

I told him it wasn't something to get right or wrong, there was only one way to do it, and that would be the way he did it. Whatever that was, it would be right. Or something along those lines. Whatever I said, it seemed to put him at ease, and he relaxed.

His friends came to visit as a group, and with each of them he met separately. With each visitor, he'd hold out his hand to shake, and he'd greet them warmly, glad to see them. He could still appreciate life while waiting, somewhat impatiently, for it to be over.

When he left us on May 31, the three of us were there, and the hospice nurse, and when he took his last breath it was as if the air went out of the room. I found myself desperately trying to clean the blood off his face as he bled out, as if he would notice, but he was already gone.

He did it exactly right.

Resources
By Stew

Finding resources for mental health is a kind of hit-and-miss activity. And even when you hit, you sometimes end up missing.

First, check your phone book for local mental health clinics/organizations. Some states, such as California, have county resources which can be very good. For me, Sutter-Yuba Mental Health in Yuba City, California, was a Godsend. There I was able to get access to a psychiatrist, Dr. Randhawa, who helped get me off some of the less useful medications, and prescribed higher doses of the good meds. And since it was in concert with the county, I was able to get things at little or no cost.

Nationally, I highly recommend the National Alliance for the Mentally Ill (www.nami.org). Through NAMI you can find local and state chapters that can assist you in finding proper therapies and doctors. In addition, they serve as a lobbying organization to help garner parity in health insurance. They also have a variety of email newsletters and advocacy forums that help eliminate the stigma of mental illness.

Local NAMI agencies can be of a great help, but sometimes they lack funding or volunteers. Please note that at the local level, many NAMI agencies are run by volunteers who themselves suffer from mental illnesses. This can lead to offices only being open for very short hours, phone calls not being returned in a timely manner, and other frustrating conditions. If your illness is manageable, you might consider volunteering for NAMI. They sure can use the support.

There are a wide variety of resources available online, but be careful. Some web sites look very well done and the people running the sites mean well, but they may dispense information and therapy when they are not qualified to do so. Make sure you realize that people are giving their own opinion and that it may or may not be applicable to you.

One web site I have found extremely useful is www.crazymeds.com. The owners of this site have been on many of the medications that are prescribed for mentally ill people, and they give their experience with them. They also have a lot of good scientific information about the drugs. But again, they are mainly talking about their experience, or the experiences they've been told about by others. Any serious questions you have should be talked about with your prescribing doctor. But it's always handy to hear how a particular medication affected somebody you're talking to.

As for therapists and psychiatrists, don't be afraid to ask questions. If you're going to see a therapist, be it an MSW, licensed clinical social worker (LCSW), psychologist — or what have you — make sure they are licensed. Ask them what kind of accreditation and licenses they have to practice therapy. If they don't have a license, run. Run fast. They can do more harm (albeit, unintentional.)

All psychiatrists are MDs. That means you should be able to look them up in your state's board of physicians and get information as to disciplinary action, when they graduated, what college they graduated from, etc. If the psychiatrist you want to see has many disciplinary actions, you may want to run. Run fast! Sometimes doctors who are more recent graduates have a better understanding of the newer meds that are out there. Doctors who have been practicing a while tend to get ingrained into old habits, and don't trust, or don't even know about the newer medicines.

If you don't think your therapist or psychiatrist is working for you, don't be afraid to say so and look for different people. This is your health we're talking about, and you need to feel comfortable with the people treating you. I made the mistake of working with a therapist for a year, realizing for six months that things weren't getting much better, before I had the strength to say, "You know, I don't think this is working." If you're not comfortable with a therapist after four or five sessions, consider finding somebody else.

Don't forget about your city/county crisis emergency number(s). Most cities or counties have a crisis line for people who are at the end of their rope. A trained counselor is at the other end of the line who can talk you down in a crisis situation. From personal experience though, I recommend that you don't say you're suicidal and then hang up. They'll trace the call and send first responders to your address. Having the cops outside of your apartment can cause even more stress, even when they are there to help you.

The ER is also a handy place to go if you're in a crisis. It's been my experience that if you go to the emergency room and tell them that you're feeling like you might harm yourself, they'll take pretty good care of you. They'll put you in safe room and soon they'll offer up somebody to talk to you. (In my experience it was an MSW.) If the hospital has a psych ward they may take you there. You can get the medication you need and possibly stay for observation.

———

So Your Loved One is in Crisis
By Stew

So you're sitting there watching an episode of "Charmed," eating a bowl of popcorn and a good friend calls you up and says: "I think I'm suicidal."

What do you do?

What happens next can be critical. It can save a life. It can cost a friendship. It's probably one of the worst things you'll have to face with your friend. But, being calm is the first step.

The first thing is to take it seriously. Suicidal people are already in a bad enough place that if you don't take them seriously, it could lead them to doing something worse to get your attention. Someone saying they are suicidal is a call for help. Don't hang up on them, let them know you're listening.

However, we all know people who are prone to histrionics. But it's best to take the suicidal person at their word, until you get to the bottom of things.

It's quite possible that are not the best person to take charge of the situation. You, too, can be an emotional wreck looking for a place to crash. If this is the case, it's imperative that you have the suicidal person dial 911, or that you do it for him. If you're in no condition to save yourself, you'll be hard-pressed to save others.

The next thing you need to do is get the suicidal person some place safe. There are a lot of options for that. The ER is probably the most severe place you can take them, but if they are an imminent danger to themselves or others, the ER is probably the best place to go. They have professionals who can help the person in crisis. If things are REALLY bad (the person has a weapon of some type) call 911 immediately. Let the law enforcement officers secure the person and situation. Let the professionals deal with it.

If the person doesn't seem to have a plan in place, but is just thinking suicidal thoughts, get them out of the situation they are in currently. If they are home, get them out to lunch. Go have coffee or ice cream with them. If they are at work, invite them over to your home. If they're in public, get them someplace private. If they are private, get them someplace public. Get them out of their current situation so they can see that there are other things happening in the world. That they aren't "stuck" where they are.

Food is a great comforter. Of course, if the person is depressed because of being overweight, food might not be the best idea. But for most people in our culture food brings back happy memories. Who can be depressed when there's a fresh loaf of bread baking in the oven? Can anybody cry over a hot fudge sundae? One caveat, however, do not encourage the use of alcohol. Alcohol is a depressant, and we don't need to depress any more of the body than is already depressed.

Water is also very soothing. Depressed people are notorious for not taking good care of their hygiene, but there's something very soothing about a nice hot shower, or a warm bubble bath. Encourage the suicidal person to get undressed and step into some type of warm body of water. Be there to wrap them up in a nice warm fluffy robe when they are done. If you have access to them, essential oils can be added to a warm bath. Some of these essential oils may have aromatherapeutic value to them. Check the web or consult an herbalist for recommendations on which scents are good for depression.

I can almost guarantee you that the last thing a suicidal person wants to do is exercise, but if you can encourage him to shoot some baskets, go for a walk, or a swim, or engage them in some type of physical activity, you'll be doing a lot for them. Exercise will get the mind off the problem, and increase endorphins which lead to the stimulation of serotonin and dopamine which makes the mind feel better. But, expect a lot of resistance. Depressed people usually don't have the energy or the stamina for a lot of physical work.

ABOUT THE AUTHORS

Monique Colver lives happily in the Pacific Northwest with her husband, Andrew, and their two well-meaning but occasionally confused dogs, Honey, who was also Stew's dog, and Ash. Honey is older now, but she's still an excellent example of a great dog with an attitude. Ash, on the other paw, is just a little bit crazy, which we find very endearing.

When not looking for an excuse to write, Monique is the owner of a boutique bookkeeping and business consulting firm. She's working on her next book, which she promises will be much more entertaining. She can be reached at Monique@anuncommonfriendship.com.

Stewart Young was laid to rest in the Puget Sound, his ashes dispersed as he wished, in the place he loved best.

Visit our website at www.anuncommonfriendship.com for more information.

www.ingramcontent.com/pod-product-compliance
Lightning Source LLC
Chambersburg PA
CBHW030009290326

41934CB00005B/271